Coaching Women's Soccer

A Revolutionary Approach to
Putting the Play Back into Practice

Ian Stokell

Contemporary Books

Chicago   New York   San Francisco   Lisbon   London   Madrid   Mexico City
Milan   New Delhi   San Juan   Seoul   Singapore   Sydney   Toronto

Library of Congress Cataloging-in-Publication Data

Stokell , Ian.
    Coaching women's soccer : a revolutionary approach to putting the play back
into practice / Ian Stokell.
        p.   cm.
    Includes index.
    ISBN 0-07-138209-7
    1. Soccer—Coaching—United States.   2. Soccer for women—United
States.   I. Title.

GV943.8 .S77   2002
796.334'07'7—dc21   2001047321

McGraw-Hill

A Division of The **McGraw·Hill** Companies

1 2 3 4 5 6 7 8 9 0   VBA/VBA   0 9 8 7 6 5 4 3 2 1

ISBN 0-07-138209-7

This book was set in Minion
Printed and bound by Maple-Vail Book Manufacturing Group

Cover and interior design by Monica Bazuik
Cover photograph © Jim Cummins/FPG

McGraw-Hill books are available at special quantity discounts to use as premiums and
sales promotions, or for use in corporate training programs. For more information, please
write to the Director of Special Sales, Professional Publishing, McGraw-Hill, Two Penn
Plaza, New York, NY 10121-2298. Or contact your local bookstore.

This book is printed on acid-free paper.

Contents

Preface

FIRST LET ME SAY what this book is not. This is not really a book about technique or tactics or systems of play. There are probably hundreds of books that can supply that sort of information.

It's more a book about philosophy—coaching philosophy. While it does feature chapters on some coaching tools and a couple dozen simple small-sided games, it's really about returning to the freegame at all levels of practice, certainly when coaching women and older girls.

This is not an academic paper. There are no references, footnotes, or bibliographies. It's more of an editorial. It's my opinion, based on thirty-five years of playing and coaching soccer. It's an opinion that's founded on a lifelong love affair with the world's greatest game, during which time I've kicked a lot of balls, made a lot of tackles, experienced more than a few bruises, watched a lot of practices, and spoken to countless players, coaches, fans, parents, and kids.

If you like, this book is also a rebellion of sorts. It's a revolution—a stand against overcoaching, too many drills, and not enough time given to just playing the game.

But what I'm advocating is little more than the freegame. The freegame is the point where the game starts and its historical splendor meets its triumphant future. It's where it all began, but watching so many practices in the U.S., it also seems so far away.

How did coaching technique and philosophy get so far from its freegame roots? Watch some coaching practices, be it club teams, high schools, colleges, or professional sides. While you're there, play "spot the freegame." You might have to wait a while, though. Coaches often seem obsessed with drills and structure, drills and discipline, and drills and "Listen to me; I'm the coach."

Where did the spontaneity go? Where is the unpredictability in players and teams that is so crucial to competing at the highest level of the game? It seems that too many coaches have become so obsessed with structure in practice and an increasingly complex array of drills and difficult-to-understand small-sided games that the game has been stripped of spontaneity and fun.

One of the major elements of a successful soccer nation that is painfully lacking in the U.S. is unpredictability in the game. That is a deficiency that sits squarely in the collective lap of this country's coaches. If we continue to drill players in practice, from the recreational leagues to Division 1 collegiate level, we'll have robots on the field when the whistle blows and the chips are down.

The reality is that soccer *does not* need coaches to survive. Coaches are not needed in the heartland of the game: on the beaches and streets of Rio where players don't even have shoes, on the school playgrounds of South London where I grew up playing with nothing more than a tennis ball and a park bench for a goal. Soccer can and will survive without drills and "clipboard" practices. Thank goodness.

In fact, I say all soccer needs to survive is the freegame.

Introduction

U.S. COMPETITIVE YOUTH PLAYERS are often overcoached, over-drilled, and overpracticed. There is too much pressure on them to succeed at all costs, often not for themselves at all but for their parents or others, such as club coaches living their lives vicariously through their players.

There are so many injuries, especially in the older girls' game. But because of overpracticing, players are getting fewer and fewer days to recuperate. And as the girls' game in particular gets more physical, injuries will only increase. As a result of insufficient recovery time, players increasingly face the prospect of long-term damage.

Club coaches could do worse than follow a simple maxim: the off-season is for fitness, the preseason is for tactical training, and the regular season is for playing the game competitively, trying to avoid injuries, recuperating from injury, and addressing whatever problems arise from game to game, with practices short and knees spared too much stress.

Year-round club teams should consider dividing the year into three or four distinct "seasons." Maybe have league play in one and a couple of big competitions in each of the others. That gives a team different times to peak, it gives players downtime through different periods of the year, and it gives players' bodies time to recuperate during long stretches of practice without hard contact.

In the U.S., coaches are still looked at as some sort of omnipotent beings. For them, everything revolves around that inflexible practice schedule, drawn up with drills and cones, grids, and stopwatches at the ready. They are unwavering in its execution—finish the schedule no matter what. Maybe the coaching mentality is brought over from established U.S. sports like football and baseball, where drills and mind-numbing repetitions are the norm.

But soccer's a different game; it calls for a paradigm shift in mentality for coaches and players coming from other sports. Because when that whistle blows on game day, there's no coach calling in plays to the field like in football, baseball, and volleyball; there's just a group of players trying to function as a team, with only on-field leadership as a guide.

Drills in practice give rise to unthinking, robotic players, unable to function without sideline coaching.

But whatever happened to the freegame in practice? Coaches usually dangle it in front of players like a carrot or dispense it like a divine right: "Give me 1 hour 50 minutes of busting your rear ends on my drills like good little players, and maybe I'll let you have five minutes of freegame at the end before cool-down." Thanks, coach. Want us to come round your house at the weekend and do your gardening for you, because we're so grateful?

What's wrong with warming players up and then giving them fifteen minutes of freegame before anything else to get the desire to just play the game out of their systems? Even two 5-a-side games is good, which gives players more touches on the ball than a full-sized game.

Also, why not let players scrimmage with a simple restriction or two instead of drilling? For example, if the team needs to work on playing the ball forward and always having a supporting player upfield toward the opponent's goal, make the restriction that players may not dribble by a defender; they may only get past a defender by passing the ball forward. If there's no support upfield, they aren't going to score.

Here's another example: if you want them to start thinking offense, have a simple restriction on a freegame of no back passes or square balls. It's amazing how much a simple restriction can influence how players think and act. Players will apply more pressure to the ball carrier on defense, as well as take the initiative to create space and attack on offense.

Everything a player does on the field requires decision making of some sort, so why have practice where decisions are taken away from the players? If shooting needs to be practiced, incorporate it into a 2 versus 2 game to a big goal with a keeper. Then progress toward integrating shooting into a large game, adding players, balls, or extra keepers. But players shouldn't be lined up like they're on a conveyor belt.

The game is the teacher. And something that many coaches seem to overlook is that players will learn from other players. They don't have to be coached every moment, all the time.

Soccer is the world's game. To play it women don't need rules, permission, equipment, even a ball. And they certainly don't need coaches around all the time giving the evil eye to anyone and everyone because they lost their "shape" at the back or didn't pressure the ball twenty-five yards out in a 5-a-side game and let a shot go in. Players will tell players what the problem is. Or the players will realize it for themselves.

Coaching soccer is about empowering players to help players and at the same time help themselves while feeling good about giving up their free time to play the world's greatest game.

Constant haranguing from coaches is the prime reason most players have left the game by the time they reach high school. And only the hardiest of teenagers will keep playing on a club team or in high school if all she gets is incessant coaching and negative feedback. There are plenty of other sports teenagers can be playing besides soccer—sports where they can have some fun. Coaches should be giving players a reason to stay in the game, not reasons to leave.

However, repetitive drills can sometimes have their place with very young players who are just learning the game and need individual instruction, but they should only used sparingly and always as a break from a freegame. However, by the time players reach the Under 13 age group, drills should be a thing of the past.

Predictable play is the death knell for competitive soccer, be it Under 15, Under 17, college ball, or professional (WUSA). And predictable play has its roots in drills that do not incorporate free thinking and decision making into practice, something all too common in U.S. youth soccer nationwide.

Some Differences Between Men and Women

WOMEN ARE NOT MEN. If that is so, which it pretty obviously is, why do so many coaches of women and girls coach them as if they are?

The main reason, of course, is that coaches have rarely been told in the past, even by U.S. coaching organizations, that there is a difference. The bottom line is that women are different, and what often works for men does not naturally work for women.

While the fulcrum for the men's game is often aggression and ego, machismo and the "me" mentality, for the women's game the fulcrum is usually much more cerebral, more naturally team-centric, and leading to a far more balanced and entertaining all-around game.

That doesn't mean that the women's game is inferior in any way to the men's game; it just means that different characteristics of the women's game are high priority. And, indeed, what follows is not an example of how the women's game is different but an example of how it's like the men's. The women's game at the highest level is now becoming increasingly aggressive—just like the men's game; you have to look no further than the 1999 Women's World Cup Nigeria versus U.S. game to see that. And in the U.S. the women's game certainly now attracts top athletes to its college rosters, whereas ten years ago that was not generally the case.

Indeed, I would argue that characteristics such as increased athleticism and a natural tendency toward teamwork mean that with some exceptions, the women's team game is much stronger than the men's. It is in men's character to be more self-serving and self-promoting than women; you only have to watch how top women athletes in team sports are more inclined to share the glory with their teammates without encouragement to see that.

However, on a superficial level, this male selfishness—the lack of concern for team unity—allows men to more easily slot into a team, at least initially. They are often more interested in their own performance than how the team is functioning. As long as things are going well, the individual players are happy to pay incidental homage to "team spirit" and "team unity." For the most part, the team comes second to their own performance. The team becomes important to such individuals only when its bad showing is impacting their performance and making them look bad.

For women, though, that desire to be part of a team, to be comfortable with their environment, and for the team to be functioning well as a cohesive unit is genuine. Once the team is working well, women players are then more inclined to move up to the next level in their personal play.

What happens when the team begins to play badly is a reflection of the differences between men and women and their gender characteristics. When the team does start to play badly, male athletes tend to melt down faster on an individual level. As they melt down, the team consciousness that had to be forced upon them in the first place is often the first casualty.

Just listen to team sports on television for a demonstration of that. It is common to hear men's team coaches and players constantly emphasizing teamwork, team unity, and camaraderie among teammates in locker rooms and on sidelines, because those are a huge deficiency in the men's game—be it soccer or football or whatever team sport is being played.

For women though, when the team and individual players are under intense pressure, it is natural for them to fall back on the very strength that is lacking in the men's game: a natural team consciousness and team unity. Teamwork is a natural foundation for the women's game. Certainly that is not always the case, and sometimes it has to be worked at, but generally the desire to be part of a team and to participate as one of a group of players is a solid characteristic of the female player.

Men could learn a lot from women's team sports, and so could men's team coaches, although many would decline to admit it in public or to themselves.

So the question remains: If the general psychological and physical characteristics of women are different from that of men, why are so many coaches coaching women the same.

The fact is that the history of soccer coaching in the U.S. is the history of coaching men players—and usually men coaches coaching men players. It is only in the last decade or so that the women's game has taken off, and really only the last six or seven years that it has exploded at the grassroots level in unison with its huge success at the top international level.

So, some would argue, U.S. women players have been successful with the coaching they have had. But perhaps they have been successful *in spite* of the coaching they have received over their developmental years, not because of it.

There's no denying the high quality of many top-level women's college coaches. And for most players, the pinnacle of their playing careers is college. But they have been exposed to ten or twelve years of youth coaching before getting to college. And much of that coaching, and a lot of college coaching (there are now over seven hundred colleges with women's soccer programs) is of, to be kind, dubious quality.

Why? Because coaches often have no concept of a difference between women and men, for one. And they rely on the time-honored, pedestrian coaching tools of the men's game: too many drills, highly rigid and structured practices, little social interaction permitted, and often their own abrasive insensitivity and all-powerfulness.

Women Want to Be Coached

Women's soccer offers a coach an extremely high-level coaching environment, not just because of women players' intelligence but also because of their willingness to be coached.

It is a coaching environment that is consistent with players of young age through college age and beyond. On the flip side it is a coaching environment that will not be a good fit for coaches who prefer to dictate proceedings with little explanation and discussion.

Generally, much of the men's game revolves around aggression and self-ego, almost to the exclusion of a team concept if the coach is not careful. Consequently, a men's team coach can find his or her time being taken up doing little more than diffusing aggressive tendencies on and off the field and placating sometimes fragile but often self-serving individual egos. There may be little time left for real on-field coaching, as the head coach becomes a personnel manager.

I would estimate that perhaps 70 percent of boys and men are, to be kind, difficult to coach. The average boy soccer player thinks he's Pele when really he possesses barely average skills.

That in itself is not a crime. The problem comes from the common male mentality of refusing to be coached to become better, in which the player thinks he cannot learn anything new. For some reason this is a phenomenon that appears to be extremely common in soccer players as compared to players of other sports, although perhaps many women would argue that it is a characteristic that extends to areas of male-female relationships off the soccer field as well!

The result is an often difficult and confrontational environment for the coach of male players, one that often can test a coach's personnel management and diplomacy skills to the maximum.

For girls and women, though, that percentile is at least reversed. I would say that at least 80 percent of female soccer players are extremely open to being coached. That doesn't mean that they want to be told what to do—in fact, far from it. That is the last thing a coach should think will work in a female soccer environment. Ordering players around with no consideration for their opinions and concerns is certainly not a good idea.

Female players want to be coached. Or to put it another way, they want to know what the coach knows, and they'll decide either to use it or not. They are usually hungry for knowledge, although only from someone whom they respect as a person and as a coach.

Again, because of the nature of women and girls, those coaching elements that can often find success in the men's game—highly structured practices, excessive use of drills, minimal social interaction between players and players and coach, tight discipline, and a dominating and vocally overpowering coach—are the very things that will turn off a women's team.

Those elements should be removed from the women's game in order for female players to reach their full potential, both collectively as a team and individually as people.

A Comfortable Environment

WOMEN NEED A COMFORTABLE environment in which they can excel. They need to be happy with their teammates, with the type of practice they are participating in, even with the practice field, and certainly with the coach. Once they have that crucial comfortable environment in which to work, they generally have no problem competing, although they are sometimes reluctant if competition is against their own teammates in practice.

Choosing Activities

Often it can be a good idea to let the players have a hand in choosing some of the activities or small games that make up part of the practice. That said, however, they should not decide what is actually covered in practice or what shortcomings need to be addressed. That is the responsibility of the coach.

Aside from encouraging player participation in some coaching decisions, it is important to leave no doubt about who is in overall control of the team and the practices: the head coach. I don't mean to say the coach always has to be at center stage. In fact, in the women's game, the more often the coach can step aside and let the natural bonding characteristics of a female team take over, the better.

Most players will have been playing for a few years even by the time they get into their teens, and they would have participated in many hundreds of practices. They will have come to prefer certain small-sided games and activities over the years. So sometimes, let them have a say as to what ones are to be used in practice.

For example, to address the lack of overlaps to the wing in the team's game, the coach would first ask the players what activities and small-sided games they can come up with or have used in their club practices in the past. The chosen suggestion can then be the starting point for the practice, to be changed and molded as the coach sees fit throughout the course of the training session.

It's best to let them have some fun and be comfortable in practice, and then take them out of that comfortable environment and test them for short periods of time with restrictions they may not have had before and activities they are not used to doing.

And it's also important to be spontaneous with practice activities as much as possible. The key to this type of coaching—incorporating player-initiated exercises and games into practices—is for the coach to integrate the elements he or she wants to address in a practice but as much as possible keep to the original player-suggested activity, at least initially. Any movement away from the suggested activity should be gradual, with an explanation that the team needs to address a certain shortcoming, and still within the context of the original activity.

This type of coaching is the most demanding. There are no clipboards to fall back on, nor any tightly regimented drills as laid out the night before in the coach's action plan for practice. With this type of coaching, the coach has to think on the fly, incorporating specific elements and techniques as he or she sees fit.

Many coaches may not be comfortable with this approach. It can leave the coach exposed and without props. However, it is also the most rewarding and invigorating type of coaching, full of possibilities but also the pitfalls of unpredictability and vulnerability.

But sometimes, involving the team in the initial selection of a practice activity is highly beneficial, in terms of both team building and having players think for themselves (without continuously looking toward the coach on the touchline for advice).

Coaches need to encourage the development of free-thinking players, those who are capable of original and unpredictable thought on the field and to make adjustments as a team throughout a game, without first thinking they need to get permission from the coach.

And women players need an individual relationship with their coach. Every player's relationship will likely be different, but every one is as important as the next. Because women are more team- and relationship-oriented than men, their individual relationships with their teammates are also important.

Fostering Competitiveness

Women are often reluctant to compete aggressively with their teammates in practice for fear of damaging the personal relationship that exists between them. They generally have no problem stepping up and competing with another team in a real game, but among teammates there can often be competitive deficiencies.

A number of college teams use a variation of a round-robin 1 versus 1 league play, for example, as a means to motivate players to be competitive among themselves. They will keep track of all scores in the matches, progressing to a 2 versus 2 and 3 versus 3, until at the end of practice a player with the most wins materializes to lead the pack. Scores and league positions are then posted on a wall for all to see.

The idea behind posting player scores and statistics is that it enables players to be more competitive and aggressive in their play without its affecting their relationships with their teammates. It is the coach that is initiating the increased competitiveness. The motivation is that no one wants to be seen on the bottom of the list too often.

Some teams go as far as having assistant coaches keep track of almost everything in practice, from successful tackles to accurate passes. At the end of practice those results are processed in a certain way to reveal a top practice player. Again, results are posted and no player wants to be constantly at the bottom of the list. The result is that players often try harder in all practices to move up the list.

There can be a definite possible benefit of such a methodology on an occasional basis—even perhaps once every two weeks. But I fail to see how such constant pressure, day in and day out, can be conducive to a comfortable, pressureless, and, dare I use the "f" word again, fun environment where players can enjoy their practice sessions and continue to love the game. Such coaching tactics will almost certainly create increased intensity in practice, which is something required if a team is to raise its game to the next level. But I would argue that constant pressure and intensity in practice is sure to burn players out over time.

And isn't soccer supposed to be fun, no matter what the level? Because if players are not having fun in practice, then what really is the point?

Again, I am in favor of creating a comfortable environment for players to train and then periodically taking them out of that comfort zone for a limited time before letting them return to it to "recover."

Involvement

Part of a comfortable environment for women players comes from being intellectually stimulated in practice. I don't mean by performing increasingly complex grid-to-grid-to-grid drills that they need a master's degree in mathematics to understand, but by being involved in the creation of an interactive practice session that addresses a given problem.

Women players need to know the context within which a particular technique or tactic fits. They will become intellectually stimulated in working together, as a team, in contributing to the way the practice seeks to address the coaching concerns of the day.

And here is a vital point in favor of the freegame coaching philosophy: having been a party to the construction of the practice, those same players are more likely to give a little more effort and create a higher intensity to make sure that the practice session works. They will try a little harder to see that the practice is successful if they have a hand in its construction than if a head coach just handed down orders from on high as to how the practice was to be carried out and what activities were to be implemented. (A "freegame" is a regular game of soccer played by two teams—the number of players can vary—adhering to standard or agreed-upon rules of play but with minimum or no supervision and no coaching.)

By involving players in the construction of a session, coaches then might not need such artificial tools as the posting of in-team scores, for example, in order to get the players to raise the intensity level of the practice.

I would argue then that, just as players do not need to be constantly harangued into wanting to win (they are often naturally competitive, outside of competing against their teammates, once they are comfortable with their practice and team environment), so players will create their own high level of intensity in practice if they are involved intellectually in its construction.

Women are relationship-oriented with regard to their teammates and to their coach. Each one wants and needs a relationship with her coach in a way that male players rarely do. But that relationship does not have to be the same as every other woman's.

And just as women generally will have no problem being competitive with other teams, they need a comfortable team and practice environment from which to step up both competitively and from an intensity perspective.

Far from being a sign of weakness, the relationship-oriented approach of women toward their fellow teammates and their coach is actually a strengthening factor in their game. It allows them the luxury of a solid foundation of team unity should things go awry on the field of play.

And that is something that coaches need to understand before they can hope to be effective in the management and coaching of a women's team.

Don't Overcoach

It never ceases to amaze me how little actual playing time many coaches incorporate into their regular practices. They spend much of their time devising increasingly complex drills, moving from grid to grid to grid, often with little real thought as to how it directly relates to a full-sized 11 versus 11 game on a full-sized pitch.

Of course, one could argue that the game is made up of half a dozen smaller games being played out in various parts of the field at the same time. But those games are never in isolation, and what happens within them is related directly to what is happening in the rest of the full-sized game and in the other smaller games going on at the same time. It's one thing to concentrate on a specific area of the game or technique and to work on that for a short time. But it is another completely to base much of a team's practice around small games and small group play, working almost exclusively within a series of small grids, rarely going to a full-sized goal with keepers in place.

It's Not Football

There is a tendency in the U.S. to view a head coach as some sort of omnipotent being who dictates everything about a soccer program, from what is eaten at the team dinner to all aspects of a practice session. This is most likely a holdover from the football and baseball mentality and comes from those coaches' moving into soccer coaching as it increased in popularity and became a huge recreational sport in recent years.

Football- and baseball-type coaching practices are likely to be unsuccessful in a soccer environment, at least when coaching women. The "omnipotent being" mentality especially needs to be removed from the mix when attempting to construct team strength in women's soccer.

Team unity is one of the true strengths of the women's game, because it comes more naturally to women than to men. Women naturally seek to share the limelight and graciously offer praise to their teammates when successful, whereas men have no problem stepping up and claiming personal glory.

Much of football and baseball coaching revolves around repetitive drills and deadball plays, quite simply because neither game has much room for spontaneous play outside of a seven- or eight-second window before the ball goes dead and the next play is called in from the sideline or dugout.

A Fluid Game

But soccer is the world's most fluid game, its most spontaneous display of athleticism, the most popular street game in the world, and the one that requires no coaching to begin playing.

Set plays are limited in soccer, and while they may occasionally be the difference between victory and defeat in a tight, evenly matched game, time spent on them in practice should pale beside time spent on encouraging free thought and spontaneity in the open field.

The idea should be to develop free-thinking players capable of unpredictable play in order to break down defenses, not robots who play the game by numbers.

From a practical sense, what is the point of spending so much time on drill-like activities when you are training for a game that is the most fluid in the world? Come game day, soccer is probably the only major team sport in which, when the whistle to start the game blows, the coach has virtually nothing to do except throw in a substitution here and there and make verbal adjustments at halftime. Virtually every other team sport has the coach directly involved in on-field plays from the sideline or the dugout. From football to baseball and softball, to volleyball and basketball, all usually involve the coach calling in plays or directing play from the sideline.

Making Decisions

Women want to be involved in team building and at least some team decisions. For example, boys' or men's team coaches would not take too much time in debating the color and design of a new team strip with their players, if any. But truly the seeds of discontent would be sown if the same happened with a female team. That doesn't make a female team any weaker than a male team; it just means that a coach should be more inclusive in some of the decision making. And such female idiosyncrasies should be viewed by the women's coach as an opportunity to strengthen team bonding and a collective team consciousness, not as a hindrance.

As is often the case with coaching women, and sometimes with men, team activities and events away from the field can prove important opportunities for a coach to build team spirit and camaraderie without taking center stage.

Coaching women requires stepping away from center stage whenever a good opportunity arises and deferring to the more common female sense of team togetherness and inclusiveness.

While a male coach's relying on the strength of his own forceful personality can be a good idea when coaching men, it can often be intimidating to women, especially to girls. Because of that, on-field leadership is probably more important to the women's game than the men's, although it is vital to both. Coaches need to let on-field inspiration come from a source other than their own personality. That's why in the freegame philosophy outlined in this book it is so important that coaches empower players to step up and take charge in practice. Having the coach dictate all areas of practice encourages players to look to the sideline in an actual game when they should be looking to one another for leadership.

Encouraging players in leadership roles in practice, by allowing them to select activities and training games for example, will pay off over time by encouraging them to step up on the field of play and take charge.

Applying Theory

And patience is a coaching virtue that is not emphasized enough in official soccer coaching certification courses. Coaches often want to see positive results from their coaching activities immediately, when sometimes it can take anything from minutes to days and maybe even weeks for players to fully grasp the meaning and context of a specific coaching element.

After a demo or explanation in practice, coaches need to give the players plenty of time to figure out how and when to apply that theory to the real game. It's all well and good to have players apply the coaching theory to a small-sided game in practice, but not exclusively, as that often gets lost when the small-sided game is applied to the context of a full-sized game. That's another reason the freegame is so important in practice; it gives players the chance to apply the theory to an unrestricted game where all the elements of a real contest come into play, from pressure to vision to movement to intellect.

So coaches need to be more patient in practice and give players plenty of time to apply the theory to a real game in their own time and not according to the coach's timetable. And once again, the game is the teacher. And it's usually a better teacher than the coach.

A coach can tell some players the same coaching point half a dozen times and it won't sink in, even during small-sided games. They will keep making the same mistake; or worse, they may not even recognize it is a mistake. But put them in a freegame and it will become painfully apparent to them.

A coach can tell a player many times and she still may not be fully listening or make the connection on how to apply it to the real game. But that same has to happen only once or twice in a real game for her to recognize the problem.

Here's a basic example. You want to make a defender understand that the first thing she has to figure out when she gets on the field is how fast the forward she is marking is. The faster the forward, the more the defender has to be prepared to play off the forward, to give her two or three yards of space ball-side when it is likely a forward pass will result in a foot chase. However, the closer to the defending goal, the less separation a defender wants to give up but the less speed is going to matter in the penalty box when there is no room to use explosive sprint speed anyway. In the open field then, defenders have to be prepared to "play off" faster forwards, dropping back an extra step or two, often marking them "in advance," in zone defense terminology.

A coach could tell a player that same thing, that she should play off the forward if the forward is faster than her, many times in practice. But it is only in a real game, when the defender gets burned, hopefully only once, where she will appreciate the sound advice and make a suitable adjustment before getting burned again.

Having bad things happen to players in the course of a real game has a far more lasting effect than telling them repeatedly in practice to adjust. Freegames in practice are the middle ground between coaching advice and a real game against real, nonteammate opponents. It may not have the full impact that a mistake against a league competitor has, but it is often better than being given a talking to by the coach.

And being able to learn by trial and error in practice freegames is indispensable for players. Practice in reading the game, as well as practice in reading the ability of opposition players in relation to their own skills, is a primary requirement at all levels of play, but it is especially necessary the higher up the playing ladder players go.

Communication

Coaches need to take the time at the outset of practice to explain exactly what is expected of the players in the coming practice session and in relation to the technique or tactic being coached.

U.S. coaching organizations often emphasize getting the players into a progression or something similar as quickly after the demonstration as possible, but that is often a mistake in the women's game. It may be true for men and the male player generally, but I would contend that it is not necessarily so for the female player.

Women's team coaches should take a pause after the demonstration and make absolutely sure that all players understand the technique or tactic being discussed and know the context in which it is to be applied in the game. Taking a couple of minutes to answer any related questions, tactical or technical, will encourage a more informed team and go a long way to creating a more inclusive practice and a more comfortable coaching and training environment.

Don't rush from demonstration to playing without a proper length of time allocated to player/coach discussion, because it will undermine the interactive and respectful coaching environment that you hope to create.

Clipboard Coaching

THE *CLIPBOARD COACHING DISEASE* is a tragic malady that manifests itself as a strange clipboardlike growth that attaches itself to one of the hands of the coach and cannot be removed until practice is over. It is caused by U.S. coaching organizations doing too much thinking about the game. Clipboard coaching creates too much structure, predictability, and unspontaneous play in U.S. soccer. This is especially true in the men's game, from youth teams up to the highest college levels and the professional and international ranks.

Clipboard coaching relies on too many drills and discipline in practice, and not enough time just playing the game. The best teaching tool in any sport is the sport itself. The game, and not drills, will teach players how to play the game. And players will learn from players.

Practice Structure

U.S. coaching organizations should take a good part of the blame for U.S. soccer's predictable play, at all levels, because of the way they emphasize to coaches on local, state, and national certification courses to keep to a certain "diagrammatic" structure when conducting practices.

Within that structure has evolved a reliance on static drills and increasingly complex grid-to-grid-to-grid small-sided games that do little to emphasize the integrated nature of having all players on the field in a full-sized game.

With regard to structure I would argue that there are two kinds: overt and covert.

Overt structure is when the coach turns up at practice with a clipboard mentality and every minute of the practice is planned down to the second, with cones ready to go, bibs lined up, and three mouthfuls of water each between activities. That may well work well for many male players, but generally, the female mentality naturally shies away from or rebels against such rigidity. Women soccer players are more comfortable in a loose environment where they can at least feel that they have some worth in the development of the session and the evolution of the team in general.

Covert structure is when the coach has control of practice and has a number of coaching points that need to be integrated into the training session over its course. There is structure, because the core content of the session—the coaching points—will be covered. To a great extent just how they will be covered, that is the activities used as the vehicle to convey them, are not always going to be set. The main vehicle will be the freegame, where players will learn from players, the game will often teach the points to be covered, everyone gets to play, and the coach integrates the coaching points at different intervals without the players' really being aware that they are being coached.

Covert structure should be the domain of the women's and older girls' soccer practice, and when appropriate—and when the players are mature enough to handle it—in the men's game as well.

Game Pressure

Whether you as a coach like to admit it or not, what you do in practice is reflected in how the team plays in the real game. If practice is set out to military precision, timed to the minute with no leeway for continuing in one direction if, for example, the players are having a good time with a particular activity, then that is how the team will function under pressure in a proper game.

You train a team the way you want them to play in a full-sized game. If players are constantly trained with drills and confining small-sided games with little or no opportunity for spontaneity, then why should anyone be surprised when they play with no spontaneity in a real game?

Part of the game of soccer is something I call *game pressure*. Players rarely feel it in training even though, one hopes, coaches would endeavor to replicate it for no other reason than to expose players to its idiosyncrasies away from a real match.

When a real game comes around and players are out on the field trying their best, myriad factors start to weigh on their shoulders, everything from playing in front of fans and parents, to not wanting to let teammates down, to wanting to play well, to feeling intimidated by opposing players. At that point game pressure sets in. And game pressure can turn a player's head to mush. She can start to forget things and, worse, she can start doing stupid things that under normal conditions she would never think of doing.

When game pressure sets in, *players revert to how they train*, not to what the coach is telling them on game day. Under real pressure they will revert to what they know. And what they know is what they practice in training sessions. Say they practice drills all the time, in which everyone has her place and they're all defending with perfect spacing and little passion for the contest. Then sure, they'll keep their shape, but they will lack the very thing that they have to come up with at the highest level of the game: unpredictability and spontaneity. And they will lack the ability to defend against it.

Teams that spend all their practices drilling under a coach's iron hand will likely compete very well against other average teams that spend all their time drilling and keeping their shape. Such a game will often deteriorate into a boring stalemate in which neither side can create scoring chances—but should a team lose, it won't be by much. And against inferior teams they will likely look good—very controlled and clinical and bland.

But overly drilled teams are easy to defend against, because they have little inspiration to do anything unexpected. And they are easy for an unpredictable team to attack. Defensively, they expect the expected because they never face the unexpected in practice. So they have no practice in compensating on the field of play on the fly.

Good, solid defense will keep you in the game, but originality and unpredictable, spontaneous attacking play will win it. That does not come as a result of clipboard coaching. And solid defense against a top-ranked team has to involve the team's ability to deal with unpredictable attacking runs from the opposition, such as those from fullbacks.

A Fluid Practice

If a team is coached with repetitive drills and constricted small-sided games that aren't treated as a stepping-off point for the freegame, they will play like robots in a real game, especially if they get put under pressure.

Soccer is the world's most fluid game, and when the match actually starts it is sometimes hard for the uninitiated to see any structure at all. This doesn't mean there isn't any, of course, and the ability of the best teams to ebb and flow with the changing points of attack from side to side is a fundamental part of the highest levels of soccer. But if players are subjected to the same type of structured practices, drills, and grid-to-grid-to-grid activities year after year, from when they are 10 years old through college seniors, it's little wonder that they play uninspired soccer.

Practices should vary in their content, from predominantly freegames to top-down progressions (see Chapter 12) to player-selected games and activities. A coach is an example, a role model, a leader, and a trendsetter. The players' attitude to the game and to a healthy competitive spirit will usually reflect the coach's. If a coach favors boring, repetitive, and drill-filled practices, then he or she has to expect the similar performance from the players on the team.

The first thing to do, then, is put the clipboard with the flow chart on how to structure a practice in the bottom drawer.

Sometimes, it will be necessary to go to restrictions and top-down progressions and simple small-sided games or other activities to get a coaching point across. That's fine. But remember that they are just stepping-off points for the freegame and that you need to vary the practice if hands-on coaching is required. And sometimes allow the players to select some of the activities for a practice.

Address Coaching Points

The coach needs to get the players involved at the outset of practice and keep them involved by allowing them to select certain activities or by petitioning feedback. But players don't have to be involved all the time, and they probably won't want to be. Even just having players selecting the stretches in warm-up will give them the feeling they are part of the team and that it is their team as much as the coach's.

A coach doesn't have to give up control of a practice when he or she seeks to create an interactive coaching environment—they are not mutually exclusive. A coach can keep control of practice and steer it in the direction he or she wants to go even when players are involved in selecting activities.

Instead of carrying a clipboard, just point out three or four coaching points that need to be addressed.

If the players are to be involved in the selection of that session's activities and it's not completely at odds with what needs to be covered, then some of their suggestions should be used. You can then, over the course of practice, integrate your coaching points into the activity or activities chosen by the players.

But teaching specific coaching points can usually be done within the framework of a freegame, using restrictions if needed. Failing that, move on to top-down progressions, small-sided games, or small-numbered freegames such as 5-a-side and sometimes to player-suggested activities.

Variety, the freegame, and fun in playing are the keys to keeping players interested in practice. And with the women's game in particular, an interactive relationship between the coach and players helps obtain a higher level of intensity in the session, which is important for taking the team to the next level of play.

Empowering Players

This is an important chapter because it goes to the very core of the freegame coaching philosophy. And it revolves around the simple question of why coaches coach the older female soccer player.

The Coach's Objective

Do coaches coach because they want to win? Perhaps they look on coaching purely as a job and think they need to win to keep their paid employment, as with a high school or college soccer team coach. Or perhaps they are club coaches living their lives vicariously through their players and the team they are coaching.

Or perhaps their idea of successful coaching is how many wins they have, to the exclusion of everything else. Too often wins are the benchmark for successful coaching, even in amateur youth soccer. Often players are pushed too hard, they are left with little time to enjoy the game and have fun, and too much pressure is put on them to *succeed*, which is a code word for *win*.

And right here I'm talking about nonprofessional soccer, such as older amateur youth and collegiate teams, because with professionals an entire new set of benchmark rules and factors come into the mix. But that's another book. . . .

So the question for coaches to ask is "Why do I coach women's soccer?" Is it a means to an end, is it the religious pursuit of the great W, or is it something more?

A similar question can be asked of collegiate women's soccer programs. Is the soccer program in place purely to gain athletic recognition for the school at the ultimate expense of the enjoyment of the players, or is it there for the good of the individual students that participate in it by helping them grow as people?

Few colleges would openly admit to the program's being there to benefit the school in terms of athletic excellence (read "wins") and therefore provide a good recruiting tool. But the reality is that some top schools seem less concerned about the day-to-day welfare and development of players and more concerned with publicity that can be gleaned from a good run at the NCAA post-season championship.

And yet any soccer program should be instigated to enhance the actual players' lives at college, adding to their enjoyment and contributing in no small part to their development as both players and people. It should help them develop qualities that cannot be garnered from nonathletic activities at college or high school, such as teamwork, collective competitive spirit, and self-discipline toward athletic excellence.

But coaching philosophy is linked, however subtly, with the ultimate goals and vision of both the head coach and the school itself. Coaching philosophy reflects both the character and ideals of the coach and the attitude of the school toward its female athletes.

And here we can identify the differences between often conflicting coaching philosophies. And although in the real world these differences are perhaps not so harshly partitioned (many things in life fall into gray areas), they do reflect an ultimate vision of why a coach coaches women. Is it for the love of the game and the development of the players as free-thinking individuals not dependent on the coach for direction in time of pressure, or for something else?

The Meaning of Success

Too often drills, discipline, and structure are the domain of the coach-centric, "win at all costs" coaching mentality.

And too many times a coach's defaulting to repetitive and static drills in training is a reflection of both a lack of real coaching ability and game knowledge and his or her identification of favorable statistics and wins as being the true indication of coaching success.

And yet, success in the women's game is often not an indication of coaching ability at all; it is a by-product of something more.

Success requires an amalgamation of factors: everything from competitive spirit to ball skills to tactical awareness, from teamwork to aggressive play, from team bonding away from the field to each individual's relationships with the coach. In addition, it should be a reflection of a coaching vision and a coach's character. It should also be the result of effective coaching.

But all too often in the women's game, it is more an indication of a team's ability to collectively rise above the ineffective coaching they are receiving or have received in their developmental years.

Sadly, although thankfully, good women's teams are often successful *in spite of* the coaching they receive, not because of it. And that can be attributed to the intelligence of women soccer players and their desire for team cohesiveness at all levels of play as much as anything.

Coaches can fake coaching ability easier in the men's game, because they can disguise their shortcomings under the character traits (or character flaws, depending on your point of view) of the male player: ego, aggression, individualism to the exclusion of a genuine team spirit, and even machismo.

But in the women's game, coaching ability is harder to fake. Those same characteristics that can be used in the men's game to disguise lack of talent, knowledge, and understanding of the game by both players and coaches are exposed as little more than props and something for a coach to hide behind when coaching women.

But in contrast, the freegame philosophy is the domain of the development coach, for whom empowering players to be more than just cogs in a winning wheel is the order of the day.

That's not to say winning is not important to the freegame philosophy. It can be, and there is nothing wrong with a team wanting to win. Team pursuit of eventual victory can build character and be extremely healthy. But as mentioned elsewhere in this book, the ultimate goal is more a question of balance.

Empowerment

A coach doesn't have to repeatedly hammer home the need to win to women athletes for them to be competitive and want to succeed. Being competitive in a team environment can come pretty naturally to many women athletes—not necessarily within their own team, as their relationships with other team members can influence how competitive they want to be in practice, but certainly when competing together against another team.

As a team, when playing another team, women soccer players will usually want to be competitive and require little encouragement in that area from the coach. The key is to create a comfortable environment from which they can step up into an increasingly competitive mindset. It will often be self-perpetuating with a women's team. Working together toward a common competitive goal is something women excel at. And a women's team requires less encouragement from the coach than the average men's team.

Individual pursuit toward athletic excellence and a collective team goal are encouraged within the freegame philosophy. But the freegame philosophy in women's soccer revolves not around drills and structure and discipline but around empowering players to be intelligent, free-thinking, self-confident, self-disciplined, team-oriented individuals ready to embrace life's challenges. Players need to be coachable, but they do not need to be robotic followers of orders.

The freegame coaching philosophy is all about empowerment. And that empowerment, which ultimately will be taken from the practice field and the soccer team and used the rest of the players' lives, is nurtured and developed within a training program of team-oriented activities that emphasize free thinking and individual intellect, as well as self-reliance and self-motivation.

The freegame philosophy of coaching is not coach-centric but player-centric. The coach is always ultimately in charge and charged with the responsibility to provide direction for the team, whether, for example, tactical or motivational. But it is also the coach's job to provide a learning environment in which the players can become empowered to think and act for themselves on and off the field of play.

Winning, Fun, and Intensity in Practice

THE NEED TO HAVE fun, that great rallying cry of recreational soccer, and the need to win, that other great mantra of competitive soccer and the collegiate game, are often both little more than excuses for bad coaching and for a total lack of understanding of the female player.

In reality, both winning and having fun are important in women's soccer. The importance of each is dependent on the level of play, the competition faced, the commitment of the players, the quality of the coaching, and in youth soccer, even the parents of the players.

Winning

For players of any age, there is nothing wrong with healthy competition, even at the recreational level, but it needs to be balanced and put in perspective. And having the desire to win, or at least not to lose, needs to be for the right reasons.

For most male players it's easy; they want to win all the time. Like it or not, it seems to be part of the male nature to want to win.

But for many girls and women it gets more complicated. Often women and girls play soccer not because they want to win or because they love competition; at least winning is not their primary motivation for playing. These women play for other, equally valid, but different reasons: everything from the desire to be healthy, to the social aspects of the sport, to wanting to be part of a team environment, to a love of playing the game.

One of the great mythical dichotomies in soccer is fun versus winning. And one of the most persistent myths about developing youth players of the game is that these two aspects are mutually exclusive. It's nonsense to assume that you can't have one if you have the other; you can have fun in playing and practice if you want to compete seriously, and you can win if you have a lot of fun. It's simply a question of balance.

There is a third element in the equation, which has a direct relation to the result and thus is itself a primary coaching tool: achieving intensity in practice. With male players achieving intensity in practice is easy; they'll beat each other up on the practice field without a second thought. But with women and girls, it's not that easy, and that is one aspect that makes coaching women harder than coaching men. A problem for coaches in the women's game is motivating them to get intense in practice, to elevate their individual level of play in order to get to the next level of team play, and to compete, at least to some reasonable degree, against their teammates. Women are relationship-oriented, and how they interact with their teammates is vitally important to them. As a result they are often reluctant to do anything that could strain those personal relationships, such as hard tackling.

Of course, the emphasis on winning is far less—some would argue rightfully nonexistent—at the recreational level than it is at, say, the collegiate level. But it is also true that the notion of fun is different as well.

Coaches should still emphasize fun at the higher levels of play, but there coaches have to be able to focus their players better.

Fun

And that great mantra of the recreational soccer game, "It doesn't matter if the team wins, so long as they have fun," although well-intentioned, is both naive and dangerous from a coaching, developmental, and player self-esteem perspective.

No matter how much emphasis is placed on having fun, nothing will destroy team morale faster than going out to play and getting resoundingly beaten every single time, by maybe five or six goals. Losing is a cancer, and it destroys morale from within. It destroys the team, which eventually, however unknowingly, looks for scapegoats and reasons for the constant pounding, and it will ultimately erode individual players' self-esteem as well. And over time that eroded soccer field self-esteem will eventually affect into the players' nonsoccer lives.

It is not OK to be constantly beaten in team sports, even at the recreational level. This is especially true if there is no visible individual or team development in which players can see a positive progression, no matter how small, toward eventually being a competitive team.

How can there be fun in practice when a team knows every time they play a competitive game against another team they will be beaten by three or four or five goals.

"We can have fun in practice because we're used to losing in our real, competitive league games." As soon as that mentality becomes the battle cry, it is time to get a new coach!

The question is not whether to have fun or to win. It's not an either-or situation. And being individually competitive is not a crime. Wanting to have fun is not a crime. The question is not whether to emphasize fun more than the idea of team competitiveness toward a common goal. The question is perhaps more one of timing.

The bottom line is that for competitive women's college programs and club teams, there is a time and a place for fun, there is a time and a place for wanting to win, and there is a time and a place for intensity in practice in pursuit of a shared team goal.

In recreational and youth soccer those three elements may all still be there, but the timing of them and their relation to each other will be different.

College Level

Let's take a look at the women's college game first.

All those elements that make women's soccer women's soccer and not men's soccer (for the better, in my opinion) come into play. The women's game of less personal ego and unrestrained aggression along with a more balanced, subtle, cerebral game where teamwork comes more naturally is coupled with the female tendency to be more relationship-oriented, more easygoing, more acquiescing, and less confrontational.

With those uniquely female characteristics in mind, where does fun fit into the college game? Where does winning fit in? And where does intensity fit in?

The best players on the best college teams will be able to have fun even at the very peak of the most intense, high-pressure competition. But that is something that good teams must aspire to; it is not something that usually comes naturally. It is the product of the highly focused athlete, confidence in both an individual's and a team's abilities, good coaching, and dare I say it, success.

But for most college teams of more limited athletic ability, on game day, it is for the coach to relegate fun to a secondary role on game day, although such an act needs to be utilized with caution in the women's game, and it should not be done without a full explanation of the reasons behind the action.

For most college teams seeking to be genuinely competitive, in whatever degrees deemed applicable, fun is for all the other times except game time, and for that matter, for game day entirely.

That doesn't mean to say there's no intensity in practice and it's all just fun because intensity in practice is essential to developing intensity in the competitive game. And that doesn't mean to say that players can't have fun in practice; in fact they should at every level.

What it means is that at certain times within practice, and certainly on game day, fun takes a backseat to intense competitive spirit and 100 percent effort. Again, the players may well be able to develop the ability to have serious fun at the peak of competition, but that will usually take time.

During a practice session of an hour and a half all the players will not maintain a high level of intensity for the entire time. There are many times when they will be able to laugh and joke within the context of focused soccer training. But at a number of times within that practice session, those same players need to be able to step into a frame of mind in which their intensity and competitiveness reaches a different level: for example, during a ten-minute 5-a-side game, free-kick run-throughs, or ten minutes of flat-4 zone defense exercises. Whatever the reason for the change of intensity level and the increased focus, players need to be able to step into that different mind-set, often at very little notice, just like they would need to do coming off the bench in a real competitive game against an opponent.

But for most women, that on-off switch for intensity has to be learned. Not many female players have the natural ability to turn it on and off in a matter of seconds. And it is learned by example and instruction. Ideally, it is developed over many years playing at the youth level, ultimately starting with a girl's first forays into recreational soccer at a very young age. Everything we do to our youth players from a coaching standpoint has repercussions, good and bad, later in their older teenage and college playing years. Mistakes coaches make at the young youth level—bad habits and mind-sets they allow their players to develop—have to be undone when those players get older. And sadly, a great many times they cannot be undone.

Recreational Level

At the recreational level, the goal should not be to win, but for the team to at least be competitive against other teams. The team should be able to genuinely compete at roughly the same level as some if not most of the other teams they face. If a team is competitive, wins will likely come eventually. That's the nature of the game. But being part of a team that is genuinely competitive builds player self-esteem and personal confidence.

At the recreational level, fun in practice and in playing should of course be paramount, but certainly not to the complete exclusion of a competitive spirit. Girls especially should be encouraged to develop a competitive attitude, at least within the context of a common team goal.

And in that respect girls often have the edge on boys because they are naturally more team-oriented and concerned with their relationship with other players, even at a very young age. So development of a competitive team spirit toward a shared achievement is healthy for them.

In one respect, it is often easy to recognize those girls who have brothers. They are more competitive in practice at a younger age because they compete at home with their generally more competitive male siblings. There is nothing wrong with developing a competitive spirit in young girls, but from a team perspective, it will be a very different dynamic from any hard-won boys' team's competitive spirit.

And in another sense, girls still have to overcome a lingering gender stereotype that says females should not have that forceful, competitive attitude that males are permitted to have. That attitude is gradually being broken down as female sports finds ever greater success in society, especially in the United States. But it is something that every coach should be aware of and endeavor to eradicate, even at the recreational level. The "it's OK to be beaten" attitude of much of women's recreational soccer, often to the complete exclusion of a team's competitive spirit and an individual's competitive spirit, only serves to reinforce that stereotype among girls and to make them accept this cultural conditioning of athletic submissiveness. And the consequences of such a development environment for girls can often be seen years later in the college ranks.

So while fun rightly should be emphasized, on a more overt level, in girls' recreational and youth soccer there needs to be some sort of balance, in which fun is coupled with the development of a competitive spirit. Its absence at an early stage can have genuine, visible repercussions for women both in collegiate athletics and in life away from the sports field.

During women's early recreational playing years the emphasis is on fun with an element of competitive spirit. In good college programs the approach is seriously competitive and focused at game time, with a large helping of fun at other times. The development path of all female soccer players must lie somewhere between these.

But I cannot emphasize enough that even at the earliest playing years, the development of a competitive spirit, however subtlety integrated into normal practice and games, should never be completely ignored in the female game.

The Game Is the Teacher

This chapter addresses two important aspects of the freegame coaching philosophy: the game being the teacher and the ability of players to learn from other players and not just the coach.

So why is practice of a technique or tactical situation better accomplished in a freegame situation than in a drill or small-sided exercise controlled by the coach?

Players Learn by Playing

One main argument for the freegame is that a multitude of game-related pressures and factors come into play in a real game that cannot be realistically manufactured using drills and limited small-sided games.

The best ball skills in the world are often rendered next to useless if the player doesn't know how to apply them to the game and integrate them into a team concept. Ball skills are not enough at a high level of play—be it club, college, or professional. Decision making and the ability to read the game and see the entire field is often just as important as good ball skills.

It is not just technique and tactical knowledge that is important; it is the application of that knowledge that can elevate a less talented player above a more talented but less thoughtful one.

In the team concept decision making and, for example, movement off the ball is often more important to the overall performance of a team than one player's ability to beat three opponents in the dribble if she never looks up to pass the ball.

Don't get me wrong. Good dribblers are a precious commodity and are generally sought out and valued by colleges, although unfortunately, often to the exclusion of players with other important skills that can contribute to a cohesive team unit. But there is more to a good dribbler than simple ball skills. She also requires skills that can be developed only in a real game under real game pressure.

The same argument is seen again in Chapter 9, which explains why drills should be banned from practices for older girls and women.

For example, the staple diet of dribbling around cones is used by many coaches to practice dribbling. But the ability to guide the ball around a set number of static markers with no pressure, outside of the context of a competitive game, can be meaningless. In the context of real game pressure, those same skills, if indeed they can be called that at all, can easily evaporate. Pressure has a way of wiping the slate of knowledge clean.

Of at least equal importance in close dribbling under pressure against a real opponent is body movement, the ability to fake out an opponent, to make her commit to an ill-advised tackle or get her moving in the wrong direction. Often that ability in a 1 versus 1 situation is more important than a deft dribbling touch with the feet.

For many players, close footwork requires them to look down at their feet, whereas an effectively played body fake (which can achieve the same result of an overcommitted defender) allows the player on the ball to keep her head up to survey the open field for passing opportunities.

Coaches need to avoid creating artificial environments in which to practice game skills. The ability to dribble, as only one example, requires much, much more than just close footwork in a small area. The skill itself is next to useless at higher levels of play unless the player has the intelligence and aptitude to apply it to the overall game and the team concept.

That knowledge does not come from drills and restricting small-sided games; it comes from practicing game skills within as close to a freegame as the intellect of the players practicing will allow.

Players Learn from Players

And within that context of the game being the teacher is the complementary notion that players will learn from players better or at least as well as they will learn from the coach.

Having a visual demonstration of a technique or a tactical maneuver is an important element of coaching—but it doesn't have to come from the coach. And allowing female players to emulate the on-field play of teammates is an important team bonding exercise.

An important element of "the game is the teacher" philosophy then is that players will also learn from other players. The two go hand in hand; emulating is the practical application of what they see other players do on the field of play.

Just as you want players to emulate the players who are good role models off the field, so you also want them to emulate those players with good skills, intelligence, and good attitude on the field.

A good demonstration or example on the field of play under game conditions will have far more impact on a watching player than a spoken explanation and a static demonstration by a coach alone will.

The most emphatic sequence for teaching women players is for the coach to explain the technique or tactic along with a demonstration, preferably by a player or two, then to have a short interactive session between coach and team in which all related questions and issues are addressed. This should then be followed by a freegame, small-numbered or full-sided, in which players who are unsure of its application under pressure can see its use on the field of play executed by their teammates.

The concept of coach-centricity in practice is, in part, almost a cultural phenomenon. Although it is not unique to the United States, there is nowhere else in the world where it is seen at such epidemic proportions.

The U.S. psyche loves its coaches' being at center stage. And this is as much a holdover from other American sports as it is the result of the infamous American male sports ego in seeking domination and self-adulation.

U.S. male soccer is still under the shadow of established and hugely popular male sports such as football and baseball, both of which, quite validly, demand the coach's being involved in virtually every play.

But for the rest of the world's youth, who have grown up playing soccer on the streets, coaches are the luxury, not the norm. For them, the freegame is not a coaching tool; it is the only tool, the only teaching aid available. For them, the game is the teacher, and they learn from their mistakes and their successes under real game pressures. The only soccer education many of them get is by watching and emulating their teammates and friends, and if they are lucky, watching an occasional professional game on television or in person.

Of course women's soccer is under no such historical constraints, because the history of high-profile and popular soccer for women in the U.S. is but a few years old. And look at the success U.S. women have had in such a short time!

But I would argue, as I have elsewhere in this book, that the success of U.S. women's soccer often has been in spite of the restricting legacy of men's soccer coaching, especially at the older youth and collegiate level, and not because of it.

Basic Practice Tools

A GOLDEN RULE FOR practice and for which practice tools to use is *keep it simple*!

Why? Because you want the players themselves to increase the complexity of their participation in the game, with, for example, crossing patterns and increasingly unpredictable runs. You don't want to stifle such innovative play by creating an artificially complex environment in the practice activity's basic framework.

You want the players themselves to make practice more complex, not you, the coach.

Half the time it seems that coaches make training supercomplex as a way of justifying their own role as coaching high priests, members of a priesthood that only a few who are deemed worthy of understanding the coaching concepts are allowed into. This coach-centric way of coaching has ruled U.S. soccer for many years.

There are some other simple, basic rules to consider, whatever the practice tools used. Soccer is a game of time and space; attackers want more time and space and defenders want to limit time and space. In practice then, pressure can be applied to an attacking team by somehow denying them precious time and space.

This can be done in a number of ways. But remember that one of the precepts of the freegame philosophy is to create unpredictable, even spontaneous, play. So don't use the same tools and restrictions each time you need to restrict time and space. Vary the restrictions used, and try not to use more than two at any given time.

One way to restrict time and space is to physically compress the space in which the practice is taking place by making the playing area in which the attackers have to work smaller. Compressing space therefore makes the defenders' job easier, while at the same time making the attackers' job harder. However, restricting the physical space in which to work will put more pressure on the attacking side only if the defense adopts a more high-pressure posture. If the defense is too low-pressure, you could halve the original playing space and still not increase pressure on the attacking side.

So in conjunction with the smaller playing area, make sure the defense is playing an increasingly high-pressure game. Also, the defense should not overcommit and get beaten in any man-to-man matchups, rather just pressure the ball whenever possible.

One point I'd like to make about high- or low-pressure defense is that the more high-pressure the defense is, the more fitness becomes a factor for defenders. And your defenders either have it or they don't. Players can try and fake it by playing more positionally, but they're just kidding themselves, because it's very easy to spot an unfit player matched up against a fit player. In a high-pressure defense, there's nowhere to hide.

And as a coach, if you have an unfit team on defense, you'll become very well acquainted with coaching positional defending!

Another way of restricting time on the ball is to reduce the number of touches a player can have on the ball. But here I would use a one-touch restriction sparingly. Often, a three-touch restriction can be a stretch under high pressure for even the best college teams. A two-touch restriction is a way to create pressure: one touch for control and one for passing. But a two-touch and especially a one-touch restriction should be used only for short stretches at a time.

A good rule to remember is the higher the pressure, the fewer touches appear to be for the team in possession. In other words, under very high pressure from the defense, three-touch play can seem like one-touch!

A more subtle way of compressing space, especially in the center of the field of play, is to make the target goal smaller. A small goal will bring more action in front of it in the center part of the field than, for example, a full-sized goal that players can shoot at from anywhere.

And here, restrictions on goal-scoring opportunities can be implemented to either add space to the field of play or restrict it even further. For example, adding the restriction that a goal can be scored only directly from a crossed ball, or a crossed ball from an overlapping wing player, will pretty much guarantee there will be a lot of width in the practice.

See Chapter 14 for more about restrictions; for now though, I'm talking about some basic practice restrictions for impacting time and space.

To work from the idea of making the target goal smaller and placing certain restrictions on the play, the simple addition of an extra player, either on defense if you want to tip the scales in favor of the defending side or on offense (called "numbers-up"), can often be extremely effective. Numbers-up on defense is going to mean the offense has to work that much harder to find spaces to penetrate. But the reverse is not necessarily so, and numbers-up on offense does not mean that the defense will work harder to defend. I think the natural tendency for an outnumbered defense is to compact around the goal and mark positionally on the outer defenses.

So while numbers-up may make the outnumbered offense work harder, it won't necessarily make an outnumbered defense work harder, just smarter, although that may not be a bad thing in itself!

So, depending on the players, a numbers-up situation does not necessarily mean an increased work rate from the outnumbered team. In fact, a rule of thumb would probably be that numbers-up on offense may lead to a lower work rate for the defense as they compact around the goal. Thus certain restrictions may be required to prevent the defense from adopting a sort of limited "bunker" defense, unless of course that is something that you want them to work on. On the other hand, numbers-up (more defenders than attackers) on defense will often force the outnumbered offense to work hard to penetrate the tougher defense.

As always with women players, explaining the object of the practice and the exercise to them and taking the time to answer any questions raised will usually prevent any unwanted defensive or offensive tactics.

Women are much more likely to buy into the specific goal of a practice as long as they are kept informed as to the purpose of the exercise and how it will help them as a team.

Having outlined some basic practice rules concerning time and space, which generally can be applied to most training exercises and activities, below I will briefly discuss specific practice tools before moving on to separate chapters covering each one. The tools to be covered are small-sided games as an alternative to drilling, freeze-frame in the freegame, top-down progressions, and the use of freegame restrictions.

Small-Sided Games

Small-sided games are important as an alternative to what I would call "static drills," which are repetitive activities whose objective is to practice a particular technique or small-group tactic in isolation, with no real decision making required from the player or players involved.

But it is extremely important to remember that small-sided games should not be a coaching tool in themselves. They are always used, as briefly and effectively as possible, as a stepping-stone toward the application of the coaching theory in a full-field, full-sized freegame.

Although 1 versus 1 activities are extremely important in any practice, I don't classify 1 versus 1 as a small-sided game in this context, because no decision making is necessary within the context of team play; 1 versus 1 merely involves the ability of one player to beat another. Small-sided games then, as I identify them, begin with a 2 versus 2 scenario whenever possible preferably to a big goal with a keeper.

Just Say No to Drills

I feel there is no place in women's soccer—and in soccer generally— for drills, especially static drills. All activities in training should involve decision making whenever possible.

Say a coach decides to practice shooting. Instead of lining players up to run at the goal and shoot in succession and then go to the back of the line, the shooting should be done within the context of a small-sided game. The coach could direct, for example, a 2 versus 2 game to a big goal with goalkeeper, with emphasis placed on getting a quick shot off whenever the opportunity presents itself in order to rotate the players and get maximum touches for everyone.

Freeze-Frame

Use of the freeze-frame approach is important because it allows for the coaching of a specific technique or tactic within the context of a real game instead of just within small-sided games or activities.

Freeze-frame is when a coach makes a certain signal within a game, stopping all movement immediately, in order to make a coaching point. All players need to be aware of the freeze signal, usually the whistle, and are to stay exactly where they are and not move out of position until the coaching point has been made.

Keep in mind two things. First, the freeze-frame approach, like all artificial practice tools, should be used sparingly, not with respect to the number of times a game is stopped, but with respect to the block of time allocated to the freeze-frame-controlled game.

Also, the controlled game doesn't have to be used as a formal precursor to an unrestricted freegame; hopefully a controlled game will very easily become a simple freegame itself, and there will be no need to stop it to make a coaching point.

In addition, just because it is a controlled game doesn't mean to say that you have to stop it. Some coaching points can be explained to the players at the end of the game.

Some coaches seem to like to stop controlled games just to hear their own voices or to let players know they are still in charge.

Second, always make sure the players know when exactly a controlled game is being initiated. And make sure they know when it has ended, if it is indeed being used as a precursor to a freegame.

Top-Down Progressions

A progression is a related series of activities with a central theme usually accomplished in a small area with increasingly complex steps. While there are a variety of ways to implement a progression, they all start out simple and gain complexity with each additional step.

For example, a progression may start with a player practicing a specific technique without opposition at walk-through pace, then at a faster pace, then with a passive defender added, then with an active defender, then move to a small-sided game with multiple attackers versus multiple defenders, and so on.

With a top-down progression though, because you are dealing with a generally higher level of intelligence and understanding in the women's game, you can start at the top of the progression and work your way down the difficulty or complexity ladder if the players fail to grasp the concept, instead of starting at or near the bottom and working your way to the top.

Restrictions in the Freegame

The use of restrictions in a practice freegame is one of the basic tools of the freegame philosophy for coaching women.

Restrictions in the freegame help players focus on specific coaching points and tactical concerns without getting bogged down with too much structure and discipline in practice.

Freegame restrictions are used as an alternative to drills and increasingly complex, restrictive small-sided and grid-to-grid activities that distract players' attention from the all-important full-field vision.

Individual restrictions within the context of a full-sized or relatively large-sized game, on the other hand, can focus the players' attention both on the coaching point at hand and on its use within the greater team concept and its physical, not just theoretical, application within the overall scheme.

Drills Should Be Banned

EVERY ACTION A PLAYER takes on the field of play requires decision making of some form or another, whether it is the simplest of push-passes for five yards or a crossing run to the near post, because no movement is in isolation on a soccer field. Every situation presents at least two options for the player to choose from: for example, to pass or not to pass, to push up out of defense or to stand her ground, to make a supporting run forward or to shadow her mark.

So if every single action that occurs on a soccer field requires decision making, why would you engage in team training activities such as drills that require no thought from the player at all? For the sake of repetition of correct technique toward excellence in execution? But no technique is ever executed in isolation; every technique occurs within a context. And that context is the game.

Repetition with correct technique placed within the correct context should be the team training environment of choice. Away from the team practice environment, personal repetition with the ball is of course required if a high level of ball skills is desired.

Free-Thinking Players

The need at the highest levels of play is to produce free-thinking
players capable of taking the initiative on the field and making on-
field adjustments as the situation demands, without needing to look
to the sideline for directions from the coach. That is increasingly difficult for players who have spent their entire youth soccer years in
practice environments in which the coach has dictated everything
about the training session and in which the actual session revolves
around closely structured drills with little room for individual decision making or innovation.

Coaches need to be aware that the name of the game is not to
develop robotic players. Discipline in team execution has its place,
of course, and a team with poor discipline has very little chance of
success.

However, execution by the numbers—always short-short-long,
always the same variation of close-in support, or always the same
post-up target forward on the edge of the penalty box with her back
to goal ready to play the ball straight back out again—will only
result in predictable, robotic players, who all have their predetermined places on the chalkboard.

What U.S. soccer needs is unpredictable, spontaneous play from
players who are not afraid to make mistakes in pursuit of innovative
team soccer, players who are not afraid to make those unpredictable
runs to the corners, and full-backs who are encouraged to attack
from the back should they want to.

But you don't get that innovative play by practicing drills in training where no decision making is required. There's nothing wrong
with repetition of correct technique, but it should be repetition
within an environment that calls for choices, options, and decision
making.

No Technique in Isolation

The line-'em-up, repetitive drill mentality works from the misguided premise that by creating such a training environment, players will be able to get more touches on the ball while focused on a single technique, shooting for example. But the reality is that most of those players are left standing around watching while someone else gets to practice the technique.

And the fact is, no technique is ever used in isolation in an actual game. To get a shot off in a real game requires that myriad complementary actions, decisions, and techniques come into play. These complementary elements range from vision in order to see the space in which to run to receive the ball, to communication between teammates, to the ability to lose a defender, to ball control in order to create the shooting angle, to faking out the goalkeeper with a subtle body movement, to name just a few. The shot itself is just the final product of many separate but interlinked parts. It is the culmination of a lot of unsung, often subtle and overlooked effort.

I associate drills with a "U.S. disease" of seeing just the final product and not the process that goes into getting to that ultimate goal. All that matters is the win, not the hard work that goes unreported in the elusive pursuit of that final act, the shot.

We put the picture of the goal scorer in the newspaper, while the player who unselfishly ran out toward the wing to pull the defender with her, creating the space for the goal scorer to run into, doesn't even get a mention.

We want more scoring in U.S. soccer so we lobby for larger goals. But what's really needed is players getting open more in scoring situations by making more unpredictable runs. Is it that we want the glory without the work? Who is to blame, the players or the coaches? Of course, it's the coaching.

Some may say I am too harsh. But once again, I'll say it: *Under pressure, players will default to how they train.* If they train to be robots, as a result of drills and too many small-sided games in isolation from the rest of the field of play, they will play like robots come game day.

Drills teach technique out of context. If a player makes a pass, then everyone on her team needs to adjust their position on the field. No one should be standing still once that pass has been made, even the goalkeeper half a field away. Nothing is ever in isolation on the field of play in soccer, so coaches should not train players like things are.

Maintain Player Involvement

Coaches should not be doing anything that encourages ball watching on the field of play. Drills with lines of players standing around waiting their turn should not be encouraged.

However, an activity in which players come off the field of play for a short rest in between participation is something else.

No player can sustain maximum effort for an entire 90 minute training session, however much they like to think they can. Letting players rest in between activities can be an important part of a training session. It allows them to focus their energy on giving 100 percent effort when they are next called on to participate, which should be sooner rather than later.

But drills or activities that require little decision making in their execution and little relevance to the ultimate full-sized game should not be encouraged.

Instead, players need to be placed in a training environment that calls for increasingly complex game-related thinking in the execution of a technique, skill, or tactic. That doesn't mean embracing the complexities of nonfocused grid-to-grid-to-grid small-sided games.

Instead, increased complexity in practice should come from the players themselves in their participation in the game.

Drills do nothing to enhance the development of free-thinking players capable of innovative play under pressure. Drills may look pretty on the practice field and efficient on the clipboard schedule for that day's practice, and they may make you look like you know what you are doing to the untrained eye. But in reality, drills inhibit the development of intellectual players capable of original and spontaneous thought.

Small-Sided Games

SIMPLE SMALL-SIDED GAMES are important as an alternative to static, line-'em-up drills. But as with all the coaching tools covered in this book, remember that small-sided games are merely a stepping-stone toward the freegame in practice.

With that in mind, however, instead of using repetitive drills in isolation from the rest of what goes on in soccer, practice techniques can often be done within the context of a simple small-sided game. For example, instead of practicing shooting at a goal via a simple line-'em-up drill, have players practice shooting within a small-sided 2 versus 2 game to a big goal with a keeper. Perhaps make the area of play for the four field players quite small to ensure some pressure on the shooter from the defense. And instead of having the field of play directly in front of the goal, it may be effective to have it off to one end of the goal to give the goalkeeper practice with the use of angles as an extra defensive weapon.

Gamelike Conditions

What a small-sided game like this does is practice myriad shooting-related skills, and not just the mechanics and technique of the perfect shot. Few shots on goal in a real game are executed under perfect conditions; there can be a multitude of factors involved, from defensive pressure to goalkeeper positioning to quality of service, all impacting the execution of the shot.

One important point to remember is that the technique, and to some extent the mechanics of an actual shot, are dictated by the shooter's ability to create a shooting angle and obtain effective separation from her marking defender. Nonperfect shooting conditions are far more likely than perfect shooting conditions, and it seems reasonable to practice for the conditions that are most likely to occur.

The ability of the shooter to adapt to the most unexpected shooting conditions is paramount. So practice under "problematic" conditions whenever possible, and should ideal conditions occur during the real game, the shooter will be more than equipped to adapt to them as well.

For the younger female player, small-sided games can be utilized as part of a progression, a midway point between the individual practice of a particular aspect of the game or technique and its eventual application within a full-sized game.

But for older teenagers and women, a small-sided game featuring 2 versus 2 should probably be the lowest level of coaching environment that is needed within the context of the freegame philosophy.

And as with a freegame, restrictions can be used to focus the players' attention on specific coaching points.

Involve the Players

Explaining to the players the purpose of the small-sided game they are about to play or the technique or tactical point that needs to be addressed should be enough for many women players to obtain a fruitful training session.

Remember that players will learn from other players if they are given the chance. So within the context of the small-sided game, make sure that the players capable of executing the technique or tactical element are evenly distributed within the various teams. This way, there is always someone on the field of play that can teach by example those players who fail to grasp the point at the outset.

As always, it is important for the coach to know his or her team. What do they like and dislike in training? If the team generally dislikes small-sided games as opposed to larger small-numbered freegames, then use them sparingly.

Or in a more likely scenario, say a group of older players is more comfortable with drills, having been indoctrinated in their use in practice from an early age. In this case it is for the coach to move them away from that toward the freegame in practice, along with the liberal use of small-sided games with fewer and fewer restrictions.

As mentioned before, what a team practices is what a team defaults to under real game pressure. A team of older players who have been drilled too much in practice throughout their youth years may have a hard time adapting to a freegame mentality, where leadership and initiative on the field count at least as much as effective coaching off it. For those teams, small-sided games, as an alternative to straight drills, can be very effective.

Using Small-Sided Games

A coach may find a small-numbered, say 5 versus 5, freegame ineffective as a teaching or practice tool for that particular session. In the freegame philosophy, small-sided games with a simple restriction or two can be used in preference to top-down progressions.

For example, after a demonstration and discussion of the specific aspect of the game to be covered in that day's practice, a coach may break the squad into two 5-a-side games. But if those games are found to be ineffective for teaching, then moving straight to a 2 versus 2 or 3 versus 3 small-sided game, with or without a restriction, may be the best and most effective course of action.

And freezing the action within small-sided games to make a coaching point can also pay dividends. Freeze-frame doesn't have to be implemented only in a full-sized game. But I'll discuss more about that in the next chapter.

So small-sided games definitely have their use, as a teaching and coaching tool but primarily as a transition step toward the ultimate goal of using the full-sized freegame in practice.

There are many examples of small-sided games in Chapters 12 through 19.

Freeze-Frame in the Freegame

FREEZE-FRAME IS THE FREEZING of all movement on the field of play following a prearranged signal from the coach, such as the blowing of a whistle. It is a snapshot of the game at any given moment in time frozen for instructional purposes.

Freeze-frame is a valuable coaching tool because it helps apply what was previously only either coaching theory or a small-sided game activity to the context of wider group play. It can be a visual demonstration of the coaching theory, but in relation to the multiple team elements that make up a soccer game.

In a sense it is the antithesis of the line-'em-up drill mentality that often, however inadvertently, takes individual technique out of the game context and puts it in isolation. Freeze-frame shows the technique or tactical coaching element as it relates to the rest of the field of play and shows individual players in relation to their teammates. In essence, it relates all the elements on the field of play to each other, whether it is a small-numbered game or a full-sized game.

No activity on a soccer field takes place in isolation; everything and everyone is connected and working together toward a common goal. Or at least they should be if they have been coached correctly. Freeze-frame should give a visual demonstration of that.

Stopping the action instantly, with virtually no further movement by any players on the field, highlights the individual elements that make up the team whole. The coach can then identify them as they relate to each other and the team objective.

Keep It Simple

And, as with all coaching, the coach should keep it simple when freezing the action.

Just one or two coaching points should be made before starting the action again. The coach should seek to focus the players' attention on the specific coaching points that are being emphasized in that practice session, even if he or she is bringing them in covertly.

The coach may see a number of errors that could be addressed. But unless they are glaring errors that need to be addressed immediately so as not to propagate bad habits, the coach should simply make a mental note or write them in a notebook, to be brought up later or at another practice session.

Drills, intentionally or unintentionally, focus the players' attention on a specific technique or tactical element in isolation. The various elements of the freegame philosophy are also used to focus players' attention on specific elements of the game. However, the difference is that in the freegame those elements are examined and practiced not in isolation, but within the context and pressures of as gamelike a situation as possible.

Just because it is a freegame doesn't mean the coach can't focus on specific coaching points and elements of play that need addressing, either with an individual or with the team.

Again, the rule is not to get too complicated. The coach must avoid having players' attention wander because they are thinking about too many new things at the same time.

This is less of a concern when coaching women because of their overall willingness to learn and be coached, but the possibility still exists.

When freezing the action it is a good idea to try to address the coaching point being made from the perspectives of different players. For example, how does it affect the right fullback's positional play as compared to the outside left midfielder's?

The coach should make sure all players and all player positions are included in the coaching discussion, although not all necessarily at the same stop, as that may take too much time. But he or she must make sure all players know their roles with regard to the coaching point being made.

Address Players' Questions

And as always, a women's team coaches need to make themselves available to answer any questions that the players may want to ask with regard the coaching point. Some questions can wait for a suitable water break or the end of the practice. But directly related questions—perhaps how a particular position needs to react under certain related circumstances—should be addressed immediately.

No player should leave that section of the practice not knowing her role on the field as it relates to the coaching point being made. If she does, then the coach is at fault.

As always, the coach should be inclusive. That is, he or she should involve all the players in the discussion and in any questions that they feel need to be answered.

Women generally like an inclusive approach to coaching and don't like particular players being left out in any way. So opening up the floor to questions relating to the coaching point only serves to encourage this team inclusiveness and togetherness.

And it's worth remembering that a coaching point made with reference to one position on the field can look very different, raising different questions and problems, from another position. How a right fullback sees a particular tactical move can be very different from how a left winger sees it.

The golden rule with using freeze-frame as a coaching tool applies to coaching women generally: Be inclusive. Involve the players in the coaching observations and a question-and-answer session. And be open to input from the players whenever possible, as long as it doesn't bog down the flow of the practice.

However, as with other coaching tools, freeze-frame should be used sparingly, and players need to be made aware of exactly when it is being used. There should be a beginning and an ending to the freeze-frame session.

And coaches should try not to interrupt the flow of a competitive freegame with an unannounced freeze-frame. If it's an announced freegame, the coach must let the players play and not interfere; any coaching observations can be held over until the end of the session.

The freeze-frame is a good coaching tool and one that can be very effective if used properly. It relates the soccer theory to the entire team concept, as long as the coach takes the time to address the coaching point from different players' perspectives. And as always with women's soccer, the coach should be available for any questions that should arise.

Top-Down Progressions

So WHAT EXACTLY IS a top-down progression?

As the name implies, it involves a progression; but because you are generally dealing with players who have a more cerebral approach to the game, you can start at the top of the progression and then work your way back down the difficulty or complexity ladder if the players fail to grasp the concept.

A progression is a related series of activities with a central theme or focus usually accomplished in a small area with increasingly complex steps.

For example, in its simplest form a progression may start with a player practicing a specific technique without opposition at walk-through pace, then at a faster pace, then with a passive defender added, then with an active defender, then moving to a small-sided game with multiple attackers versus multiple defenders. Whenever possible it is best to finish a progression with going to goal in some form or another.

There are a number of variations in how to go about accomplishing a progression, but they all share a straightforward element:

start simple and add complexity or pressure with each additional step.

How far to go back down the different levels in a top-down progression when, for example, moving over from a restricted freegame is of course up to the coach. And here the key is for the coach to know the players on the team. How "soccer smart" are they?

The premise of a top-down progression in this context is that because it involves women and older female players, you don't need to go all the way back down to the simplest lower levels. However, that said, I'm sure there are many men's teams where top-down progression would work as well. But generally speaking, top-down progressions will be most effective with female teams because of a willingness to be coached and to learn—to cite just one of many favorable coaching factors.

But however smart the coach thinks his or her team is, a coach has to be responsive to the needs of the players. They may seem very intelligent, but even smart players have times where they fail to grasp the simplest of instructions.

At this point remember a basic premise of the freegame philosophy: Players will learn from players. Usually there are at least one or two players who will understand what is being demanded of them by the coach, and they can be used to educate the rest. And that education will usually be by example.

Remember to make sure the few players that understand the concept are used in a demonstration for the rest of the team.

Women players especially will willingly learn from other players, perhaps not overtly but certainly through emulation. That can be an indispensable and very important coaching tool. And that is why it is important to empower players to step up in their actions both on and off the field of play. When given encouragement on the field and in practice to give her input by both the coach and fellow players, a player who is shy off the field may step up to become an invaluable team leader and a useful coaching assistant.

Again, another important freegame philosophy premise needs to be considered; the coach needs to create an environment in practice and within the team where players feel comfortable enough to both step up physically and mentally and feel that their verbal contribution is worth something. And as always, they need to not feel self-conscious about running the risk of making a mistake in practice, especially when trying something new.

When to go to a top-down progression and how far the coach needs to go down the complexity level ladder varies from situation to situation, team to team, player to player.

Of course, a golden rule is for the coach to know his or her team and not try too hard to force artificial coaching tools, such as progressions, on to the team if they are not comfortable with them or if they will respond better to alternative coaching methods like a small-sided game or a small-numbered freegame such as 5-a-side.

As already mentioned, what happens if the team does not respond well to freegames? That is probably the one instance where the coach should get them used to freegames no matter what, but by using alternative training methods such as small-sided games and eventually small-numbered games, such as 5-a-side. Within the soccer environment I would argue that the freegame is not an artificial coaching tool the way a progression is. It is the "natural" environment for soccer. It is the one main soccer environment where coaching is not required to play the game.

But if a team collectively is not comfortable with the freegame in practice it is almost certainly an indication that they have been over-drilled and overcoached in their youth playing years; surely a crime that no youth player should have to endure, but one that too many coaches are guilty of.

The use of the highest levels of top-down progressions—with a little more structure and more rules than a small-sided game, 2 versus 2 for example—can be used as a way to get a team more comfortable with less structured, game-oriented training tools such as the freegame. It can also be used as a way to teach players who are already comfortable with the freegame concept.

So the basic guidelines for when to use a top-down progression vary from team to team, coach to coach. As with all coaching tools, top-down progressions need to be used sparingly, as an adjunct to the freegame and not a replacement. The freegame is the soccer environment that players should be most comfortable with.

As with any additional coaching tool, top-down progressions should not be used every practice. They should be utilized to teach a specific aspect of the game and then discarded for a more realistic practice environment with more gamelike conditions.

Knowing their players is a must for coaches. Coaches must know what their players like and don't like and when they will respond best to the use of top-down progressions in understanding a specific aspect of the game.

Figure 12.1 is an example of a simple top-down progression.

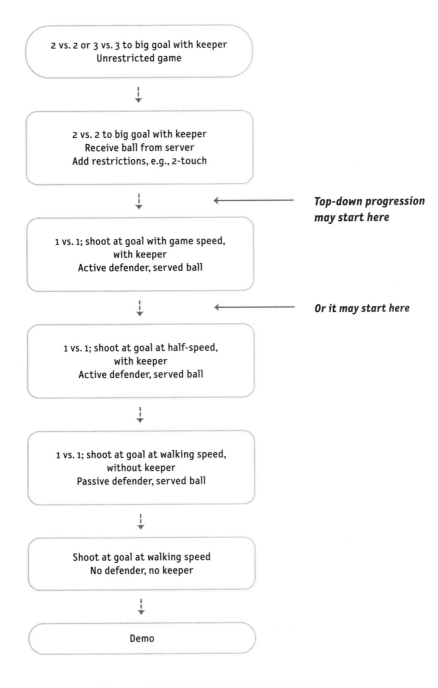

FIGURE 12.1 SHOOTING PROGRESSION EXAMPLE

Patterns and Shadow Play

USED SPARINGLY, PATTERNS AND shadow play can be important tools in the freegame coaching arsenal. Both methods essentially "paint a picture" of how certain elements of the game should look on the field of play. Once that picture is understood by all players, the next step is to implement it within a game context, possibly at the small-numbered freegame level, such as with a 5-a-side, but as quickly as the players can grasp it at the full-field freegame level.

Typically, *patterns* are used to show how players interact with each other toward a common short-term objective, such as moving the ball from the defense out to the wing and then down the outside channel into the attacking third or a midfielder's overlapping a forward to get into space in the corner of the field.

Care has to be taken when using patterns, though. The overuse of patterns bears a frightening resemblance to using drills, which need to be avoided in the freegame approach to the game. The difference between patterns and drills can be a fine line. The idea of patterns is not to produce robotic players but simply to imprint in the players' minds what a correct tactical situation or player inter-action looks like on the field of play.

Shadow play, on the other hand, is just what it sounds like. Like shadow boxing, it involves playing against an imaginary, passive, and then nonpassive opponent. Shadow play is most often used at the initial stages of explaining a new tactical approach or style of play or system. For example, it would be used for a team moving from a purely man-to-man-with-sweeper defense to a more zonal approach.

Combining Shadow Play and Patterns

Shadow play and patterns can often be combined to great effect in imprinting a particular style or tactical approach in players' minds.

For example, the paragraphs that follow detail how you might use shadow play and patterns in explaining to a team how to move the ball from the right fullback to the right corner in the attacking third. Teaching a team this skill might first entail a verbal explana-tion, a "written" explanation on a chalkboard, or a demonstration with cones on the ground in front of the assembled team, followed by a physical demonstration in a small area and then on the full field.

At that point, run some half-speed patterns on a full-sized field but using just the defensive half, preferably using all the team in rota-tion to give everyone an idea how to recognize the threat defensively as well as offensively.

Because this is shadow play, there are no defenders, at least not initially. If at all possible, always have a forward in position in front of the goal finishing from any crossed-ball exercise. Finishing and scoring are, after all, the whole point of the game, so give players as many scoring opportunities as possible.

In addition, always have goalkeepers playing in the goal as much as possible. They too need as much full-field, big goal practice as possible.

The next stage of pattern play and shadow play is to move up to three-quarter speed and finally to full speed. The object of patterns and shadow play is to get the players familiar with the soccer element being worked on and then move them onto a full-field game where they can implement it in real time, under real pressure.

Once the players are suitably comfortable with the element being practiced and comfortable at a high speed, the next phase is to bring midfielders and then defenders into the shadow play. Do this over a full field to get the entire team used to the element's execution in a full-field, full-team environment. An alternative is to keep the practice within a localized context, for example, just the attacking third of the field, and to introduce defenders.

Initially, as with the introduction of defenders to any progression, the initial step would be to introduce a single defender or two defenders but have them play a passive role. In other words, they are not trying to win the ball or even to get in the way of the ball.

Once the players are comfortable with the presence of defenders in the exercise, the defenders can begin to elevate their intensity. Hopefully this will culminate in a full-speed, full-intensity defense that gives the offense a serious workout, both physically and mentally, that is, decision making at full game speed under pressure.

The introduction of defenders into full-field shadow play is the same: add one or two passive defenders, probably around the target players, who gradually increase their speed and defensive intensity. Gradually introduce other defenders across the field until the offense is attacking a goal defended by a full-numbered defensive unit.

It is important to note, however, that while it is the ultimate goal of shadow play and patterns within the freegame concept to move on to an unrestricted full-field freegame as quickly as possible, that transition to the next stage should not be forced. If the players are not fully understanding what is being taught, then slow down, explain it again, even take a step back down to the previous level, removing the defenders if need be.

Don't Be Afraid to Slow Down

Speeding through to the next level in pursuit of the ultimate freegame is extremely counterproductive if it is at the expense of a complete understanding by all the players.

Women players generally want a full understanding of what is being coached before moving on to the next stage. Coaches should embrace that inquisitiveness because it makes for a better team with better execution and often indirectly bonds a team further.

Coaches should not succumb to the typical male player's desire to forget the full explanation and move on to the playing part as quickly as possible, even at the expense of understanding fundamental elements of the game! Generally speaking, males just want to play and are not too concerned with coaching or learning new elements of the game. I believe this is true even when none of the players understand what the coach is talking about and therefore cannot teach the players who don't understand by their example on the field of play.

Full-field, full-team shadow play is usually a good culminating short-term goal if shadow play is being used as a coaching tool. That said, however, coaches do need to move the practice on to a full-field freegame as quickly as possible because full-field, full-team shadow play inevitably renders many of the players being left uninvolved directly with the ball or the attack.

And surely, a secondary goal of any coaching is to involve as many players as possible directly in the practice. If the full-field, full-team shadow play practiced is focused on the winger moving into the strong-side corner in the attacking third, for example, then the weak-side backs will be left twiddling their thumbs for much of the time.

That is unless the coach encourages the use of wing-back attacking runs on the blind side, which, of course, he or she should.

So patterns and shadow play are an important coaching tool, but only if used sparingly, in a focused manner, and as a stepping-stone to the freegame. The different stages of both patterns and shadow play need to be addressed only as long as it takes for all the players to understand the coaching point. Keeping the training session going in a fluid manner should be the major consideration, always moving briskly toward the culmination of any practice: the freegame.

Freegame Restrictions

THE GOLDEN RULE FOR practice also applies to using restrictions in the freegame: *Keep it simple*. Restrictions should focus players' attention on specific aspects that need to be addressed and not overly tax their brains with just trying to figure out where they need to be on the field of play. As mentioned before, the idea is for the players to voluntarily increase the complexity of their game themselves, and not for that complexity to come from an artificial practice environment created by the coach.

At any point, the conventional restrictions on time and space can also apply to the freegame as well as small-sided games; for example, decreasing the size of the playing area, decreasing the number of touches on the ball, increasing the number of defenders in relation to the number of attackers (numbers-up) or vice versa, decreasing the goal or target size, or making the defense apply high pressure.

That said, however, for a full-sized game on a regular field, restricting the playing space is not really an option, as it defeats the purpose of playing a full-sized game in the first place. So when utilizing a full-sized field, any restrictions that artificially keep the players from using the full width of the field should be avoided. The practice session should make use of the entire playing space a full-sized field offers, leaving restricting the playing area size to small-numbered or small-sided games.

Certainly, dividing up a full-sized field into theoretical channels—left, center, right (see figure 14.1)—and into thirds—defending, midfield, and attacking (see figure 14.2)—can be highly useful coaching tools. One reason they are useful is that they relate directly to individual player positions and team positions on the field. But they don't place out-of-context constraints on the practice the way small grids often do when used excessively.

An entire book could be devoted to just examples of freegame restrictions and small-sided/small-numbered games as they address specific issues. But what follows are just a few examples of freegame restrictions, plus a couple of small-sided games that can be used to focus player attention as a precursor to the freegame. More small-sided games follow later in the book.

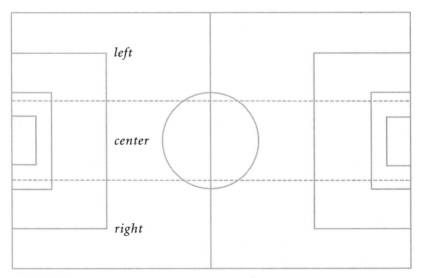

FIGURE 14.1

I must repeat here that it is important not to spend too long with the same restrictions in any freegame. The purpose of the restrictions is to focus player attention on what is required from a soccer perspective.

So keep it simple, and try not to use more than two restrictions, three at the most, at any one time.

Remember, one size does not fit all. Restrictions are placed on the freegame to address specific deficiencies or problems. If, for example, the team is not having a problem getting players forward in support of an attack, then the coach should not place related restrictions on the freegame. The coach should just tell the players to keep doing a good job.

Even though positive feedback can be extremely important in the men's game, it can be doubly effective in the women's game. This is because, generally, it is in the nature of women players to try to please their coach by attempting to carry out the coach's on-field instructions. Positive feedback makes women and girl players feel

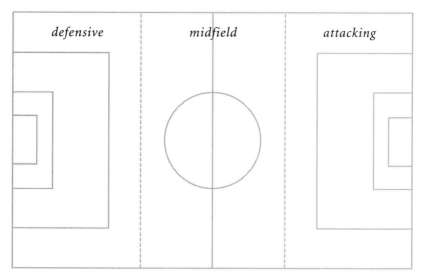

FIGURE 14.2

better about themselves and will usually lead to their putting even more effort into the practice.

Many of the restrictions listed in the examples in this chapter can be used to address multiple coaching points. However, the cliché "variety is the spice of life" rings true in soccer practices as well; the same restrictions should not be used all the time. When thinking up restrictions, the coach needs to focus on what is required of the players; more width in attack, for example, will likely require at least one restriction involving the outside channels in some way.

What follows are six examples of problems that a team may have to work on in practice, along with two small-sided games. For each problem, I have listed a number of restrictions that can be applied to a freegame to help a team overcome it. The restrictions can be used alone or in combinations. As always, use any given restriction for only a few minutes at a time as a way of focusing players on overcoming the identified problem, for example, lack of width. Then return to a straight freegame to see if the restriction has helped them focus on the problem and overcome it.

Problem 1: First Passing Option Always Forward

These restrictions are intended to get players to think of an attacking option as the primary one rather than simply playing it safe the whole time, using a possession pass with no thought of an offensive or penetrating move.

Restrictions on the Freegame
- No passing backward.
- No passing square (used mostly in conjunction with no passing backward).
- Only players upfield can audibly signal; there should be silence behind the ball carrier.

- No dribbling across the halfway line with the ball; ball has to cross the halfway line as a pass or long pass.
- No dribbling at all.

The last restriction could be dangerous, as dribbling into space is an important offensive element, so use it only occasionally and then for short periods of time. But it does make attacking support move more in order to get separation from their marking defenders and keep the attack going.

If you really want to see what a team is capable of, use no dribbling at all along with no passing backward and no passing square. They will really have to work to retain possession of the ball. To get the intensity level into the stratosphere, have the defense apply high pressure when using the no-dribbling restriction.

Problem 2: Width in Attack

Lack of width is a huge problem in U.S. soccer. The restrictions can be used in isolation or in pairs. The restrictions also address different width-related problems, such as no width in supporting runs from the back when on offense, or the lack of switching the ball across the field during an attack.

Restrictions on the Freegame
- Ball must cross the halfway line in an outside channel.
- Forward must receive a ball in the outside channel, in the opponent's half of the field.
- Goal must be scored directly from a crossed ball coming from an outside channel.
- No attempt on goal until a switch has occurred from one outside channel to the other in opponent's half of the field.
- To emphasize build-up from the midfield, ball must be dribbled across the halfway line in outside channel.

- To emphasize long ball offense, ball must be passed over the halfway line in outside channel.
- To emphasize buildup from the back, a full-back must either dribble the ball across the halfway line in the outside channel, or be involved in an overlap in an outside channel but in the opponent's half of the field.

Problem 3: Support Moving Forward

These restrictions are intended to emphasize the need for supporting runs when attacking. They focus on supporting runs coming from the back or support coming from the opposite side of the field as a result of a switched ball.

Restrictions on the Freegame
- Only an overlapping player can take the ball over the halfway line.
- A goal can be scored only as a result of a first-time cross from a supporting player overtaking the ball carrier, although not necessarily overlapping.
- Only a player receiving a switched ball from one outside channel to the other can pass the ball into the attacking third.
- Goals can be scored only directly from a cross from an outside channel, and only full-backs can cross the ball.
- Before a goal can be scored, the ball must be played to a central midfielder in the opponent's half who is in the central channel. That midfielder must then play the ball to a supporting attacker in the outside channel opposite where the original pass to the player came from. If the pass came from the central channel, the midfielder can choose to go to either outside channel with the next pass.

- Before a team can score, when the ball is played across the halfway line to an attacking player in the opponent's half, that player must hold the ball and can immediately pass to a supporting player coming across the halfway line only *after* the ball does. Once that initial support pass is made, the attack can continue unrestricted.

Problem 4: Transition

Transition is a key part of the game of soccer, so much so that there is a separate chapter, Chapter 19, on transition later in the book. These freegame restrictions emphasize the need to be ready to transition from attack to defense at any given moment, the use of width and outside support in transition, and the need for quick team support upon a transition opportunity.

Restrictions on the Freegame
- Change of possession on the whistle. This is an excellent restriction for a game of any size, from 11 versus 11 to 3 versus 3.
- When the whistle blows, the ball carrier becomes first defender and there is immediate transition, with the entire team moving to a defensive posture.
- On winning the ball in the defending half, the ball can cross the halfway line only when at least one attacking player gets into each outside channel. A further requirement would be to specify that the attacking players have to be in the opponent's half, or even in the attacking third (if slow buildup from midfield is the order of the day).

See Chapter 19 for a full discussion of transition and related small-sided games.

Problem 5: Handling High-Pressure Marking on the Ball

This high-pressure example is an excuse to include one of my favorite small-sided games: a possession game in which four defenders have to stop two attackers from passing the ball to each other in a small area. Skills learned in this tough small-sided game can definitely be applied to a full-sized freegame, especially where a long ball offense is favored.

With regard to the freegame, the best way to practice handling high pressure is probably to have the defense apply constant high pressure and have a suitable number of substitutes on the sideline that can be rotated into defensive positions when the onfield defenders begin to run out of gas.

Adding additional defenders is also a good way of putting additional pressure on the offense.

Restrictions on the Freegame

- Numbers-up in defense (two extra defenders, for example) but extra defenders allowed to stay only in defensive end.
- Numbers-up in defense; extra defenders must double-team attacking forwards at all times.
- Defenders aggressively apply high pressure to attackers in defensive third, or defending half depending on fitness level. Have extra defenders ready on the sideline to rotate in when field players get weary.

Coping with high pressure on the ball can be achieved with a restriction in a freegame—such as adding extra defenders—or through a small-sided game that can be used as a precursor to a freegame. A small-sided game can also be used as a progressive coaching step should the simple restriction in the freegame fail to accomplish the necessary learning goals.

This double-team element can also be applied to a full-sided freegame, either by double-teaming specific players by adding an extra defender on the field or by adding extra defenders to the game without a specific double-teamed player in mind.

Guide to Diagrams

——————→   *Path of the passed ball*

- - - - - - - - - →   *Path of player running without ball*

· · · · · · · · · ·▸   *Player dribbling with ball*

(**K**)   *Keeper*

(**N**)   *Neutral player*

Figure 14.3
2 vs. 4 IN A SMALL GRID

This small-sided game helps get players used to fending off a high-pressure double-team while maintaining possession.

In a medium-sized grid (at least to start with) four defenders have to stop two attackers from making five passes to each other. If the defenders manage to win the ball, the two defenders have about thirty seconds to get it back. If successful, the repossession by the two attackers counts as a single pass and they continue with their five-pass objective. Few attacking players will last more than thirty seconds trying to regain the ball from four attackers. The game is called if the attackers run out of steam trying to get the ball back before the thirty seconds is up.

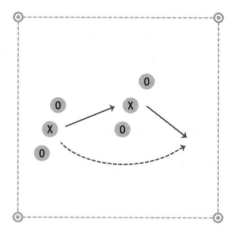

FIGURE 14.3

The size of the grid depends completely on the ability and mental strength of the two attacking players. Restricting the playing space will make it harder for the two attackers to find open space to receive the ball; making the playing space larger, (that is, making the grid bigger) will make the task of five passes slightly easier.

Until all players get used to the intensity and physical requirements of the game, start with no tackling from the defenders; they are to merely contain the attackers and steal the ball should the opportunity arise. Once the players become used to the game, let the defenders tackle the two attackers.

Coaching Points for Attackers
➤ Communicate.
➤ Generate lots of movement off the ball.
➤ Fake movement and disguise intent.
➤ Attackers should follow their pass for quick return.
➤ Head for space to receive.
➤ Play the ball to space for the second attacker to run onto.

Problem 6: Shooting
(with emphasis on making chances)

These restrictions address a variety of shooting problems, such as taking too long to get a shot off once the team has penetrated the attacking third, not taking enough shots outside the penalty box, and not taking the responsibility to shoot once they receive the ball in the penalty box.

Restrictions in the Freegame

- Time limit on attacking team to shoot or the ball turns over once the ball moves into attacking third or opponent's half.
- Points system for goals scored, with more points for shooting from outside the penalty box.
- Points system for both goals scored and shots taken.
- Anyone receiving the ball inside penalty box must shoot; no passing inside penalty box.
- First-time shot only inside of penalty box; no passing or second touch.

Meanwhile, the small-sided game that follows (figure 14.4) addresses the problem of not creating a shooting angle once the ball is played to an attacking player in the penalty box. After one or two restrictions focusing on this problem have been attempted in a freegame without success, the practice could move on to this focused small-sided game. After a suitable amount of time is spent addressing the problem in this smaller area, move back to the freegame .

Figure 14.4
OFFENSE/DEFENSE INSIDE LARGE PLAYING AREA

Attacking players are Xs.

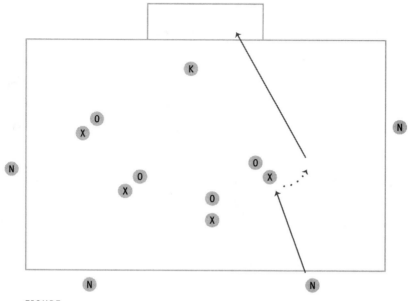

FIGURE 14.4

➤ Use large grid with one big goal and keeper.
➤ Set number of attackers and defenders playing tight man-to-man marking such as 3 versus 3 or 4 versus 4.
➤ Any number of servers placed around the edge of the grid.
➤ Servers, in turn, play the ball into the attacker with best separation from marker.
➤ No passing. Instead, receiving player must turn and shoot.

This game involves fast and constant service. It's an extremely strenuous game when played at full speed.

Coaching Points
➤ Generate movement before the pass to get separation from marker.
➤ Look to see where the marker is before receiving the ball.
➤ Check back for the ball.
➤ Turn away from the marker and shoot quickly.
➤ Serve the ball crisply to feet of attacker.

(15)

Width and the Outside Option

THERE IS A PAINFUL lack of width in much of the U.S. game, from weekend recreational games to youth competitive clubs, to top colleges, to professional WUSA teams. To be sure, lack of width is the Achilles' heel of U.S. soccer.

And yet width in offense adds a whole new dimension to an otherwise constrained and restricted attacking scheme. Width and the threat of a switched play open up the entire field to be exploited and utilized by any team with full-field vision.

And the outside option should not just be reserved for the attacking third of the field. The outside option in the defensive third can alleviate trouble in the form of high pressure on a ball-carrying fullback or sweeper. The outside option needs to be a fundamental weapon in the arsenal of every player and every team.

It's difficult to say why much of the U.S. game, especially at the youth level, girls and boys, lacks width. Perhaps it is the result of coaching by people who have moved over from other sports and do not have an instinct for the entire spectrum of the game. Perhaps it is just the result of coaching by people who have grown up on the game but not as played in a fluent, spontaneous freegame style. Whatever the reason, many coaches simply don't know how to integrate width into practice, other than through ineffective drills and training sessions.

Thus, you could say the lack of width in the U.S. game is a by-product of too many restrictive drills, a lack of innovation and spontaneity, and reversion to the same predictable, uninspired play that is so easy to defend and contain.

Width is important because it opens up space in the center for ball carriers or supporting attackers to penetrate and exploit. Width adds a necessary dimension to any attack. Width provides a way to circumvent compact defenses with diagonal balls and weak-side runs, fast switching play, and diagonal, corner runs from a central forward to receive balls played down the line.

But developing width-oriented teams doesn't come from static practice drills.

To repeat, under game pressure, players will revert to how they train. If they usually have the option of a sweeping long ball switch in their practices and the space to play wide in order to get more time and opportunities to penetrate, with or without the ball, then width in attack will come naturally in the real game. As I have said, there is sometimes a need to move away from the freegame in order to fully explain to players particular aspects of the game. But those forays into small-sided games and top-down progressions should be short and concise. And as soon as the players seem to grasp whatever conceptual point the coach is making, the return to the freegame should be as quick as possible.

What I call "natural width" comes as a result of freegames in practice and the coach's encouragement to play wide. Given "permission" by the coach and an expectation by their fellow teammates, women players especially will revert to wide play in attack. Women players will almost always try to do what their regular coach and their teammates want them to do. If there is always an expectation that they need to be playing wide, then women players will generally try to fulfill that expectation.

What I would call "artificial width," a result of forced drills in practice, will result in artificial width in the real game. Artificial width in attack is present under good attacking conditions. But it will be lacking under pressure and when things are not going well— just when a team needs it most.

Width as an attacking tool begins in the defensive third of the field, sometimes as a result of thrown distribution from the goalkeeper. Or it might be the result of an outside fullback's dropping back toward the corner on the edge of the penalty box to offer herself as an easy path out of pressure for an inside fullback, the sweeper, or even the keeper.

Width, and especially width as a result of attacking runs from outside fullbacks, works as an offensive tool because it always causes the defense to slide over in some way to compensate for the outside run. Good things are far more likely to happen on offense when a defense is forced to slide left and right across the field than when the defense is allowed to set its defensive shape in stone and not have to move far to mark attacking players.

Make the defense work to be effective. Make them move. Make them run. Make them think and communicate. Test them at their most vulnerable points, which for way too many teams in the U.S. game are on the outside and into the corners.

The outside option will get a player out of trouble. It will create attacking opportunities that would otherwise not be available. It will spread the defense and make them work. It will lead to entertaining soccer.

And talking of getting in and out of trouble, I always think of the creative, attacking use of width and the outside option as being the antithesis of much of the current mentality in coaching today, which sees possession almost as an end in itself. This is in spite of logic that width and the outside option are a means to maintain possession and possibly open up scoring opportunities at the same time. Many coaches today automatically assume that a cure-all answer to problems on the field is to emphasize maintaining possession of the ball: "Ball possession will cure whatever ails ya." Keeping possession of the ball, in much of world soccer, not just the U.S., has turned into the top priority.

But possession is not an end in itself, even though watching professional soccer around the world—and especially in the U.S.—you wouldn't know it. Possession is just a means to an end, with the end being to score a goal and ultimately to obtain a suitable result. It was never an end in itself—until the modern game.

Today, in much of the U.S. and international game, soccer has deteriorated into a glorified game of keepaway, where short passes, often a dozen at a time, are used to move the ball up the field barely ten yards on offense.

There are many excuses for such a painful approach to the game. One is the intense pressure on professional and college team head coaches as well as competitive club team coaches not to risk losing the game through too much offense and therefore leaving a team mistakenly exposed at the back.

But equally so, argues the purist, surely at some point those fans who come to watch the professional and college game must be taken into consideration. Who wants to watch a team that never gets a shot off at goal or that spends five minutes on the ball to move it twenty yards upfield?

Let's set aside professional players, whose financial responsibilities inevitably bring added pressure to the mix. Surely youth players and most college players are entitled to enjoy the game they are giving so much of their valuable time to play. And enjoyment doesn't just mean robotic possession of the ball with no penetrating runs, or merely twenty ten-yard passes in succession.

If the coach has done his or her job and the team has an effective defense, why should giving up possession of the ball be such a big deal? It would only be a problem if the defense is suspect. And if the defense is suspect then the coach is ultimately to blame.

Solid defense coupled with inspired and unpredictable offense is a recipe for success. But possession for the sake of possession is a recipe for boredom and for defeat, at least in the long term, both on and off the field.

Of course the development of the zone defense has also helped close down entertaining offense. It is effective and efficient when executed well but extremely boring to watch and frustrating to play against if all the forwards are accustomed to executing by-the-numbers offense with little width or outside play.

If anything, the effectiveness of a well-executed zone defense, whether four or three at the back, makes an even greater case for the need for inspired, unpredictable, innovative play from the attacking team. Inspired play by the attacking team is needed in order to shake a well-organized defense, and both width and the outside option must play a vital part in that vision.

Lack of width in attack and possession for the sake of possession are two disturbing elements that are increasingly common in the U.S. game. Both problems would be greatly relieved by a healthy dose of the freegame in practice and encouragement from the coach, in both words and practice activities chosen to prepare the team for competition.

What follows are five small-sided games that focus on developing width in attack. As always, use them only as a stepping-stone to the freegame. (See "Guide to Diagrams" on page 89 for an explanation of the symbols.)

Figure 15.1

3 vs. 3 *or* 4 vs. 4 WITH NEUTRAL PLAYERS ON FLANKS

This game involves the classic use of outside channels. Because goals can be scored only from a cross, the attacking team is constantly looking to either outside channel to pass the ball into. Width then becomes an integral part of the offense.

➤ Xs have possession to start.

➤ Playing area is medium-sized with two outside neutral channels.

➤ 3 versus 3 in large center channel, with two neutral players in the out-side channels who are always on offense.

➤ Use big goals with keepers; score when the opportunity presents itself.

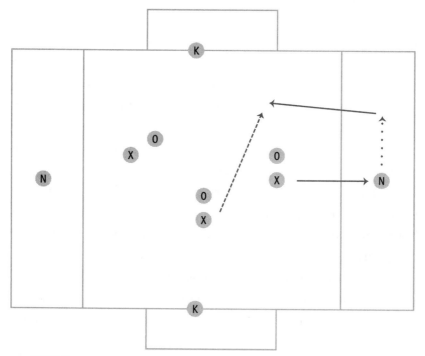

FIGURE 15.1

➤ Attacking threesome can score only with their heads or a volley directly on a cross from neutral player in outside channel. No other players are allowed in outside neutral channel.

➤ Immediate transition on change of possession.

Coaching Points

➤ Generate movement to create forward pass opportunities.

➤ Get ball quickly to advanced outside wingers.

➤ Crossing runs by attackers in front of goal.

➤ Attackers should hold off on their runs into scoring positions in front of the goal until they see from the winger that she is ready to cross.

Figure 15.2

3 vs. 3 IN EACH HALF WITH SUPPORTING RUN TO CREATE A 4 vs. 3

This game is highly effective for creating width in attack. When the attacking team moves into the opponent's half, an extra attacker can come across the halfway line with the ball, which creates a numbers-up scenario on offense. A basic rule with such a numbers-up on offense is use both outside channels to spread the fewer defense players in order to create gaps that can be exploited.

➤ Xs have possession.

➤ Medium-sized to small field is divided into two equal halves.

➤ Use 3 versus 3 in each half; use two big goals with keepers; and score when the opportunity presents itself.

➤ When attacking 3 versus 3 manages to pass the ball over halfway line to teammates in attacking half, one of those players can cross over the halfway line to create a 4 versus 3 to goal.

➤ Immediate transition on change of possession during play.

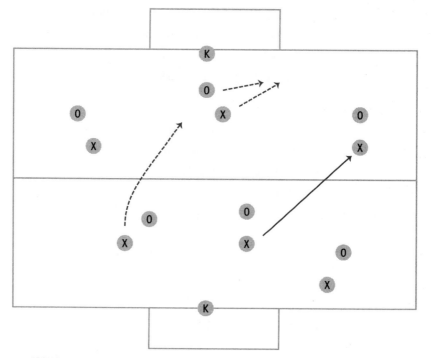

FIGURE 15.2

Coaching Points

➤ Generate movement to create forward pass opportunities.

➤ Target players work to get separation from markers or to create space for a supporting attacker's run.

➤ Attacking runs from the defensive half should be into space or to the flank in attacking half.

➤ Numbers-up on offense; spread the defense with runs and passes to the flanks.

➤ Create outside passing options to force the defense to slide over.

Figure 15.3
6 vs. 4 DEFENDING BIG GOAL

This is a more realistic "full-sized" game, where the four defenders must compact and defend the goal and at the same time pressure the ball, while the six attackers can really work the wings to exploit their numbers-up. The attackers must really spread the ball wide to start with and use an outside option and overlapping runs to gain the upper attacking hand.

➤ Xs have possession.
➤ Play in defensive third of full-sized field or larger.
➤ Six attackers play against four defenders.
➤ Use big goal with keeper; score when the opportunity presents itself. One or two targets on the forward edge of playing area for defenders to clear to.

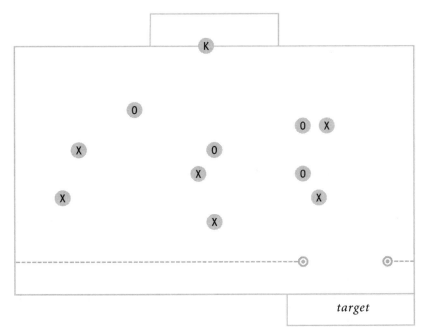

FIGURE 15.3

➤ Six attackers try to score on the big goal. Four defenders try to prevent the score and if possible win the ball and clear it to the designated target area.

Coaching Points

➤ Generate attacking movement to create space for passes or runs.

➤ Target players work to get separation from markers or to pull defense out of "shape."

➤ Numbers-up on offense; spread the defense with runs to the flanks.

➤ Create outside passing options to force the defense to slide over.

➤ Be patient on both defense and offense.

Figure 15.4
3 vs. 3 IN EACH HALF WITH
SUPPORTING RUN TO CREATE A 4 vs. 3

This game can be used on a field of any size right up to the full-numbered 11 versus 11 freegame. On offense the ball must pass through one of two sets of cones on the halfway line in the outside channels. The game encourages width and an outside passing option to get over the halfway line, or switching the ball to the opposite side of the field if the near side is well defended.

➤ Xs have possession.

➤ A field of any size is divided into two equal halves.

➤ To be used in a freegame or small-sided game.

➤ Use any number of players (3 versus 3 in each half through 11 versus 11 game); use big goals with keepers; and score when the opportunity presents itself.

➤ The ball has to cross the halfway line between two sets of cones placed on the halfway line, one on the touchline and one five yards in from the touchline.

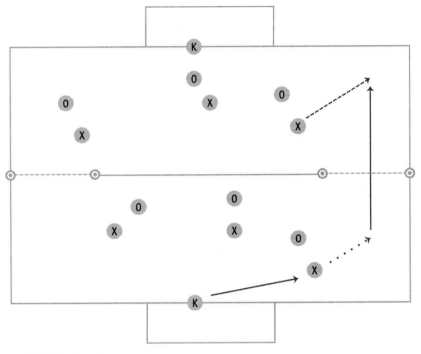

FIGURE 15.4

➤ Extra element: having to *either* pass through cones or dribble through cones.

Coaching Points
➤ Generate quick movement of the ball out of the defensive half into the outside channel.
➤ Provide run support for the ball moving out to the wing to secure possession as it crosses the half.
➤ Attacking players need to be in position for the switch across field should one cone target be closely defended in numbers.
➤ The faster the forward motion of the ball to the flank, the less time the defense has to set up and defend either crossover point in numbers.

Figure 15.5
THE USE OF CORNER GRIDS FROM WHICH CROSSES
MUST ORIGINATE

The use of corner grids from which crosses must originate is a simple restriction to be used in a game of any size, although it is oriented toward a larger number of players. The requirement that a goal can be scored only from a corner grid cross encourages wing play, overlapping runs, and an outside passing option to get into a scoring situation.

➤ Any sized field is divided into two equal halves.
➤ Any number of players, usually equal teams, usually big goals with keepers, score.

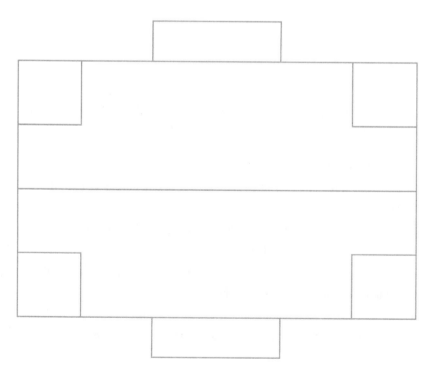

FIGURE 15.5

➤ The attacking team must cross the ball from one of the corner grids marked off with cones.

➤ An alternative is to specify that the ball must at some point enter one of the attacking corner grids before the offensive team can score.

➤ The small grids can also be moved back from the goal line, so they are midway between the goal line and the halfway line, with the stipulation that the ball must move through one of the grids in the attacking half before a goal can be scored.

Coaching Points

➤ Support of the ball as it moves through the designated grid.

➤ Provide short and long offensive support on the attacking side of the grid to give the ball carrier or receiver the chance to keep the forward motion of the attack going in the right direction.

Attacking Fullbacks

FULLBACKS SHOULD BE used as an integral attacking weapon for any team. But for a long time in U.S. soccer they have been used primarily in a defensive role. This has started to change in recent years and will hopefully continue.

Major attacking opportunities are overlooked when fullbacks are not used in an offensive role. Fullbacks don't have to stay in a defensive role throughout the game. Even used sparingly it can create opportunities up front for not just fullbacks going forward, but for forwards and midfielders moving into the attack.

It is a crucial role of the forwards not to just try to score but to create space in the attacking third for their teammates to exploit. This is primarily done through unselfish, off-the-ball running by the forwards that draws their marking defender (if it's a man-to-man marking defense) or their temporary chaperone while they are in a specific zone (if it's a zone marking defense) out of position slightly. This creates space, however small, for a supporting attacking player to exploit, either by running into it herself or by playing a ball into the space for a teammate to run into.

This constant off-the-ball running is a game-long attempt to make the defense lose its shape on the one hand and create exploitable space on the other. However, losing team shape is not necessarily a problem in itself unless there is a supporting attacker there to exploit it and the ball carrier has the vision, dare I say the full-field vision, to take advantage of it.

But not all space is bad from a defensive standpoint. Sometimes space is offered to the attacking team when you want them to go in a certain direction, toward your stronger defenders for example, or toward the sidelines. Space is also offered by a zonal defense when the attacking team is given considerable space on the weak side of the field, away from the ball, where a defender marks an attacking player moving into the weak-side zone "in advance." In the latter zonal example, the space is closed down only when the ball is switched to the weak side, which promptly becomes the strong side, and all defenders slide over to the new side to oppose the new point of attack.

Sometimes the defense will give up space in the outside lanes if the team chooses to compact around its goal or pack the center channel in front of the goal. Such a scenario of course is made for the attacking wingback, who overlaps the conventional winger or wide midfielder either to receive the ball in the corner or down the line, or to make a blind-side run toward the back post in order to be on the receiving end of a cross from the opposite sideline.

Forcing the play to the outside and then containing the ball carrier so no cross can be made is a common defensive practice. One main alternative is to force the ball inside where covering defenders are waiting. Major problems in forcing the player with the ball wide, and therefore away from the dangerous area in front of goal, include keeping the ball in the outside channel and not allowing the cross and not allowing a supporting attacker to overlap or a ball to be played into the corner. Both raise the serious possibility of the attack getting behind the defense.

As with all soccer though, the key to success lies in the execution of the theory on the playing field. If your right or left back can't cross the ball, it's probably not a good idea to use her as an attacking wingback!

But the space created by forwards or midfielders in the attacking third through off-the-ball running can be exploited just as easily by fullbacks as it can by midfielders. And in many cases it is preferable to send a fullback into the space instead of a midfielder.

Midfielders will generally either have a marking defender/midfielder assigned to them, as in straight man-to-man marking, or be easily picked up by a zonal defender when they enter a defensive zone. In both defensive systems, sending up a fullback instead of a midfielder can create problems. The attacking player must be part of a coordinated attacking scheme involving one or two or three other players whose job it is to create confusion with their off-the-ball running and to drag defenders away from the intended point of attack.

In a straight man-to-man defensive system, a fullback can be sent forward, particularly on the weak-side wing with the ball attacking down the opposite side, for example, with the hope that the defending midfielders will be too busy either watching the attack develop or concentrating on marking their assigned attacker, thus failing to pick up the blind side run.

Most important, defenders need to prioritize the attacking players in terms of the most dangerous threat on their goal. If an attacking fullback is coming through the defending midfielders and into the attacking third, either the sweeper needs to pick up the penetrating player or one of the defending midfielders needs to drop off her midfield mark and pick up the threatening player. The other defending players then prioritize the remaining attackers, again marking those that pose the greatest threat to goal, and moving accordingly.

One reason for sending up a fullback instead of a midfielder into forward-created space is that fullbacks generally do not have an opposing defender assigned to them per se, other than perhaps a forward adopting a defensive role. Sending up a fullback can create confusion or can result in that player being open because of a blown marking assignment, with one of the defending midfielders not dropping off her midfield mark to cover the attacking threat. Fullbacks are much more likely to find themselves open, particularly with wide weak-side runs, than attacking midfielders are.

On the flip side, when a fullback does make an attacking run deep into the opposition's defending third, a midfielder has to recognize what has happened and drop back into the fullback's role to ensure complete defensive coverage. If the attacking fullback cannot get back in time after the attack has finished, especially if it involves a quick non-dead-ball change of possession, the covering midfielder then must assume the defensive position of the attacking fullback until there is a suitable time in the action to make the switch back. The attacking fullback, meanwhile, will then temporarily take over the defending midfielder's role and regular marking assignment.

Sending a fullback into the attacking third against a zone defense can also pay dividends. This works if the attacking fullback is, again, working with her teammates to stretch the defense wide, allowing for less covering play by the defenders in adjacent zones. This also works if the attacking run of the fullback loads up a single defensive zone with two or three attackers at the same time, with the intention of causing confusion or a blown marking assignment.

With a zone defense, defenders will mark a designated space and man-mark any attacker that runs into that area, instead of marking a specific player the entire game, as in straight man-to-man marking. Of course, zone marking becomes man-to-man marking when an attacker moves into the defender's zone, but the attacker is usually handed off to the defender in the next zone once she moves out of the first defender's designated covering area.

Most important, attacking fullbacks also give width from the back. They can stretch an otherwise compact defense in the attacking third. They can also cause confusion about who on the opposition's defense picks up their penetrating run; thus a fullback can find herself open and in a goal-scoring position in the proximity of the goal or possibly create more space for other attacking players to exploit.

But the key for attacking fullbacks is innovative, unpredictable runs into vulnerable defensive spaces. Learning to recognize such potential runs and execute them effectively comes primarily from freegame practice and not by incessantly repetitive drills. That said, however, painting a picture with coaching tools such as rehearsed patterns and shadow play is important in order for the players to recognize the situation in the heat of competition.

Many of the small-sided games in this book can be adapted to utilize an attacking fullback as a featured element of the attacking or scoring portion of the practice.

The first three small-sided games featured in this chapter can be used on their own or as part of a three-stage progression to gradually get the players familiar with opposing defenders adopting attacking roles and responsibilities. There are many variations on these games.

The fourth and fifth small-sided games in this chapter are variations of the same game. The fourth game is an offensive game with the defense simply clearing toward targets if they gain possession of a live ball. The fifth, though, includes a second big goal with keeper to practice immediate transition from offense to defense for the attacking team, as they must backtrack at speed to defend their goal should the wing-oriented attack break down.

All in all, these five small-sided games are intended to encourage defenders to join the attack. (See "Guide to Diagrams" on p. 89 for an explanation of the symbols.)

Figure 16.1
2 vs. 2 WITH SUPPORTING RUN TO CREATE A 3 vs. 2

This is the simplest of small-sided games, where a 2 versus 2 in each half allows for the creation of a 3 versus 2 in the attacking half, with the forward movement of a defending player when the ball crosses the halfway line.

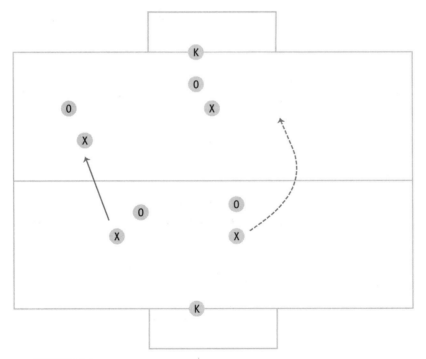

FIGURE 16.1

➤ Xs have possession to start.

➤ A field of any size is divided into two equal halves.

➤ 2 versus 2 (or any equal number, such as 3 versus 3) in each half.

➤ Use big goals with keepers; score when the opportunity presents itself.

➤ When attacking, the 2 versus 2 in the defensive half plays forward pass to teammates in the attacking half and one attacking player can cross from the defensive half into the attacking half, creating a 3 versus 2 on goal.

➤ Immediate transition on change of possession.

Coaching Points

➤ Generate movement to create forward pass opportunities.

➤ Target players work to get separation from markers or to create space for defender's run.

➤ Attacking runs from the defensive half should be into space or to the flank in the attacking half.

➤ Numbers-up on offense; spread the defense with runs to the flanks.

➤ Look for an outside passing option to force the defense to slide over.

Figure 16.2
2 vs. 2 WITH SUPPORTING RUN ACROSS
NEUTRAL ZONE TO CREATE A 3 vs. 2

This small-sided game is similar to the previous one except there is a third zone of play to cross: the neutral zone. This encourages a longer forward and accurate pass by the defenders and more movement in support of the ball from the back.

➤ Xs have possession.

➤ A field of any size is divided into three zones, with the center zone neutral.

➤ 2 versus 2 (or any equal number, such as 3 versus 3) in the end zones.

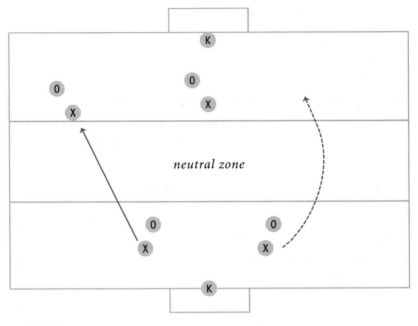

FIGURE 16.2

➤ Use big goals with keepers; score when the opportunity presents itself.
➤ When attacking in the 2 versus 2 game, the 2 versus 2 in the defensive
  end zone plays long forward pass across the neutral zone to teammates in the attacking end zone, while one attacking player can follow
  the ball and cross the neutral zone from the defensive end zone into
  the attacking end zone, creating a 3 versus 2 on goal. The size of the
  neutral zone depends on the ability and fitness level of the players.
➤ Immediate transition on change of possession.

Coaching Points
➤ Generate movement to create forward pass opportunities; fitness
  becomes an issue.
➤ Target players work to get separation from markers or to create space
  for defender's run.

➤ Attacking runs from the defensive half should be into space or to the flank in the attacking half.

Figure 16.3
2 vs. 2 IN THREE THIRDS WITH SUPPORTING
RUNS TO CREATE 3 vs. 2

This small-sided game encourages more supporting movement from defending players into attacking positions. As the ball is played forward into each of three zones, an attacking player can cross into the next zone with the ball, always creating a numbers-up situation on offense.

➤ Xs have possession to start.

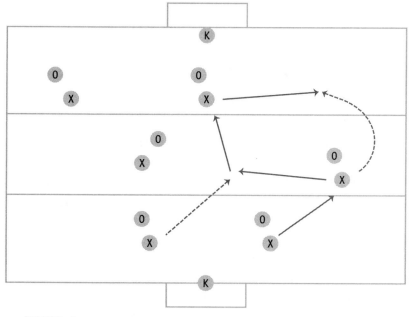

FIGURE 16.3

➤ A field of any size is divided into three zones, with 2 versus 2 in each zone.

➤ Use big goals with keepers; score when the opportunity presents itself.

➤ When attacking, 2 versus 2 plays forward pass to teammates in the next zone, and one attacking player can cross into the next zone as well, creating a 3 versus 2.

➤ Maximum of two defenders in any zone.

➤ Pass must be to the next zone.

Coaching Points

➤ Generate movement to create forward pass opportunities; greater full-field vision is required.

➤ Target players work to get separation from markers or to create space for defender's run.

➤ Initially concentrate on attacking runs being into space created on the flank in next zone.

➤ When beginning from the defensive third, try to have fullback cross into each zone.

Figure 16.4
2 vs. 2 IN 3 ZONES WITH SUPPORTING RUNS WIDE

This small-sided game puts emphasis on not just supporting runs from the back, but supporting runs out wide. The use of attacking wide support runs from fullbacks is extremely useful in the full-field, full-numbered game, as it adds another dimension to any offense.

➤ Xs on offense to start.

➤ 3 zones with a neutral channel running their full length on both sides.

➤ Use a big goal with keeper at one end and 2 targets for the defensive clearance at the other.

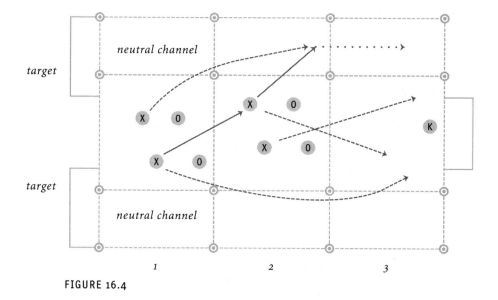

FIGURE 16.4

➤ 2 versus 2 in both zone 1 and zone 2; attackers in zone 1 play ball forward to teammates in zone 2.

➤ Both attackers from zone 1 make overlapping runs to the outside neutral channels.

➤ Both defenders from zone 1 drop back immediately to zone 2 and create a 2 versus 4 in the center channel with defensive numbers-up.

➤ Receiving attacker in zone 2 quickly plays the ball to one of the overlapping attackers, who moves into zone 3.

➤ All other players collapse back into zone 3 to try to score (attackers) or to defend.

➤ Defensive team clears to targets should they win the ball.

Coaching Points

➤ Use speed in overlapping supporting run to the flank from the fullbacks.

➤ Use speed in laying off the ball in zone 2 as the 4 defenders seek to regain possession.

Figure 16.5
2 vs. 2 IN 3 ZONES WITH SUPPORTING
RUNS WIDE AND TRANSITION

This small-sided game makes variations on the previous one, one of which is
to replace the defensive target with a second goal to create attacking and
finishing realism in transition should the defending team win the ball.

➤ Xs have possession to start.
➤ One of many variations on this game is to remove the targets and put
  in another big goal with a keeper.
➤ If defense gains possession of the ball, they go immediately to the
  other goal; attackers then immediately backtrack in transition mode.
➤ Use big goals with keepers at both ends.

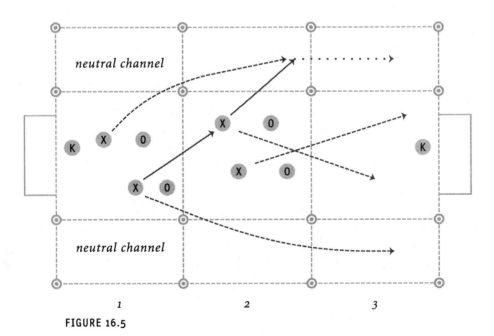

FIGURE 16.5

➤ Upon initial attackers' losing possession, the neutral channels are removed and it becomes a freegame to score in the respective goal.

➤ Another variation is to remove the neutral channels from zones 3 and 1 for the attacking team to allow for the numbers-up defense to close down the cross more effectively.

Coaching Points

➤ Offense goes to immediate transition upon loss of possession.

➤ If there is no neutral channel in zone 3, focus on speed at which defense can close down the cross.

The Long Ball
and Full-Field Vision

THIS IS ONE OF THE most important chapters of the book because the long ball is so key to a truly balanced game. This is true for men's soccer, but is especially true for the women's game, where the lack of an accurate long ball is a such a major deficiency, particularly in the United States. A *long ball* is a kick that travels anything over twenty-five to thirty yards depending on the level of play, usually driven quite hard so it gets to its destination quickly and accurately.

The Long Ball

Thankfully, little by little, season by season, use of the long ball in the women's game is growing. More coaches are becoming aware of the long ball's benefits throughout the youth level. Probably more important, increasing numbers of players are becoming aware of its value as they try to get into the better women's collegiate programs.

But make no mistake about it, players do not acquire an accurate long ball overnight, and women cannot get an accurate long ball in one spring training; it takes years of development as a youth player, not just to develop the muscles, strength, and technique necessary to deliver the pass but to develop the mental capacity to know when to play it.

The ability to deliver the long ball is of little practical use if its partner in crime, full-field vision, is missing from a player's armory. Just as any pass lacks completion without the passing player's movement after it, so the long ball sits in lonely isolation without the full-field vision necessary for its effective execution.

Typical examples of the accurate long ball's benefits to the team game include switching the point of attack from one wing to the other, immediate transition from the defensive third to the attacking third, and the ability to relieve defensive penalty box pressure without the cleared ball falling to an attacking player and therefore coming immediately back.

The relief of high pressure with a switched long ball and the switching of the point of attack from one wing to the other into space can work well together in turning a stifled attack under danger of loss of possession into an immediate attempt on goal. Such a scenario would not be as effective if the accurate switching long ball were missing and in its place were two or three shorter passes. Such a two- or three-stage switch, of course, would give the defense an extra few seconds to slide across to cover the weak side of the field as it becomes the new point of attack.

It is worth noting, however, that all pressure is not necessarily bad pressure, as long as it is the attacking team dictating the pressure's location on the field. The war cry "Play out of pressure" is often heard from the sidelines, but an element often overlooked in coaching is how an opponent's pressure on the ball carrier can work in the attacking team's favor, providing the offensive team maintains control of the situation.

Continually passing the ball from player to player in the face of threatened defensive pressure is fine if you want to merely keep possession of the ball, frustrate the opposition, or simply bore spectators to death. But offensive passing needs an ultimate purpose other than simple possession if it is to be truly effective.

An attacking team drawing defensive pressure to one wing opens up the field on the weak side for the possible isolation of a defender and the creation of a 1 versus 1 to goal attacking situation. A fundamental element in such a scenario is the intelligent use of the accurate long ball switching pass.

Such an attacking scenario is made even more effective when the attacking team can lure more defenders close to the ball and away from the protection of the goal. As with all double-team or small-space defensive numbers-up situations, especially on the wing, the greater the numbers-up disparity in favor of the defense, the greater the possibility of an attacker's pushing forward and being open away from the immediate action.

Certainly a defensive numbers-up situation of one attacker against two defenders in an outside channel is a promising start to an attack. But a close-in 2 versus 3 scenario out wide is even more enticing, and a 3 versus 4 is even better. The more defenders involved in a small-space defensive encounter, especially on the wing, the better.

The point is to get as many defenders to commit to the confrontation as possible before the switching long ball takes place. Numbers-up on one side of the defense often means the possibility of an isolated, 1 versus 1 defender somewhere over to the weak side, especially if attacking fullbacks are used.

But the accurate long ball is not simply a useful tool to switch the point of attack from one side of the field to the other.

Using the long ball in the defense, which is so essential to European-style play such as with a 4-3-3 system, not only turns defense into offense instantly but it immediately puts many of the previously attacking players on the wrong side of the ball upon losing possession. And whenever that happens, a continued speedy advancing attack condemns them to playing catch-up as the long ball offense goes to goal as quickly as possible.

Full-Field Vision

In all these scenarios one thing is clear: the accurate long ball is effective only if the ball carrier has the full-field vision necessary to recognize offensive opportunities as they develop. The long ball and full-field vision go hand in hand.

From a coaching perspective, there is nothing like full-field freegames for developing full-field vision. For example, the full-field vision involved in the use of short passes before playing the break-out long ball to the weak side of the field is as vital as an accurate, long ball defensive clearance to alleviate pressure.

Full-field freegames can also be substituted with "full-width" freegames, where the long ball is still an option and where specific group play needs to be isolated and worked on.

Defensively, for example, when implementing or practicing a zone 4-4-2 or 4-3-3, it is effective coaching to use just the defensive third or the defensive half with the fullbacks and the midfielders defending against a varying number of attackers in a freegame-type exercise. As the defense gets more adept at handling attackers moving from zone to zone, increase the number of opponents and ultimately the complexity of their runs and movement. Having two small goals on the halfway line touchlines gives the defense a long ball clearance target if they can win the ball.

And that full-width but limited length (up and down the field) approach can be used for practicing in the middle third and the attacking third while still allowing the long ball to be used from one side of the field to the other. How the midfield prevents penetration by the opposition and how they can effectively mark and close down the passing options can all be covered with a full-width, limited length playing area. Targets can be used for both offense and defense, for example, with the offense crossing a specified line across the field or the defense scoring into a small goal.

Big goal targets should be used wherever possible for the offensive third and maybe even for those in the midfield, as it gives perspective, adds realism, and gets players used to scoring with accuracy and the correct touch.

Full-width playing areas, such as the entire defensive third, also help teams with lateral movement, from both a defensive and offensive standpoint. It more effectively helps them compact correctly, either to the strong side in a zonal defense or around the goal and penalty area, for example. It also helps with switching the point of attack and playing the correctly weighted long ball under some sort of opposition pressure.

Full-field vision is something that must be developed over time, because it has to become instinctive. Under pressure with little time to react or think, players need to be able to select the best option, whether short pass, combination play versus a defender, dribbling with the ball, or playing the diagonal long ball switch behind the defense. You cannot teach such vision in a single preseason. Instinctive play cannot be obtained overnight.

In this day of stifling zone defenses and increasing female athleticism generally, which directly leads to higher pressure on the ball, the long, accurate ball is so vital. It should be practiced and encouraged at every opportunity, and time should be taken at training sessions whenever possible to improve its accuracy and strength, such as during the initial warm-up stage.

What follow are five small-sided games to encourage the use of the long ball. (See "Guide to Diagrams" on p. 89 for an explanation of the symbols.)

Figure 17.1
LONG BALL PASS/1 vs. 1 IN THE MIDDLE

This small-sided game is a warm-up exercise to encourage the use of the long ball pass.

➤ Os have possession.
➤ Four players: two playing 1 versus 1 in the middle with two on the outside.
➤ Outside player plays ball to the feet of the attacker, who must turn and play the long ball to the other side.

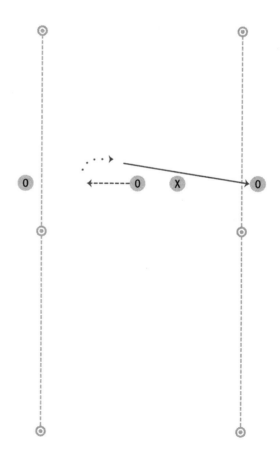

FIGURE 17.1

- If the 1 versus 1 pressure from defender is great enough to prevent the long ball, the attacker plays the ball to the player who passed it in and she plays the long ball to the other side.
- The defender then becomes the attacker, and the attacker in the middle becomes the defender.
- Change over the two in the middle for the two on the outside after a set amount of time.

Coaching Points

- Edge players serve the ball in firm to feet only when called for by the attacker in the middle.
- Attacking player must work to get some separation from the defender so she can turn, so she must be ready to check back for the ball and call loudly when ready.
- Concentrate on the long ball being hit crisply and accurately along the ground to feet.
- Immediate transition to defense/offense.

Figure 17.2
LONG PASSING/FOLLOW-UP SUPPORT

Long passing/follow-up support is a possession game intended to encourage the long ball out of pressure followed by movement of all attacking players in support of the long pass.

- Os have possession to start.
- Play is on two same-sized grids next to each other.
- Two neutral players are on the outside each end of grid.
- 4 versus 4 or 5 versus 5 in one grid; all players in one grid.
- Attacker plays the ball to the neutral player at the far end of the other grid.
- All players follow into the other grid after the long ball pass.

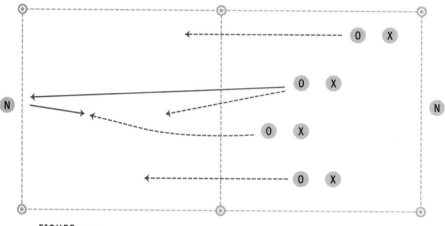

FIGURE 17.2

> Point is scored if the neutral player can pass the ball to a supporting attacker coming over from the other grid, but it cannot be the player who made the long ball pass.

Coaching Points
> Provide close passing support to create the long pass opportunity to the other grid.
> Generate immediate movement in support of the long pass.
> Look for immediate width from attacking players crossing into the grid to receive the return pass.
> Defense must be patient and work to close down the forward long pass opportunity.

Figure 17.3
LONG PASS/IMMEDIATE SUPPORT

Long pass/immediate support is a possession game featuring two neutral players who are always on offense. The long ball between grids is followed by supporting runs by the neutral players.

➤ Os have possession.

➤ 4 versus 2 in the end grid with the ball; 2 versus 2 ready in the opposite end grid.

➤ Two neutral players are always part of 4 versus and always on offense.

➤ In the 4 versus 2 game there must be five passes before players can play a long ball to a teammate in the other end grid.

➤ Once that ball is received at the other end grid, the two neutral players cross the neutral grid and make a 4 versus 2 again.

➤ Change neutral players after a couple of minutes.

➤ Immediate transition upon ball loss.

Coaching Points

➤ Provide close passing support to create the long pass opportunity to the other grid.

➤ Generate immediate fast movement in support of the long pass across the neutral grid.

➤ Look for immediate width from attacking players crossing neutral grid.

➤ Defense must be patient and work to close down the forward long pass opportunity.

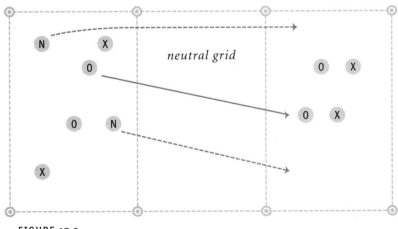

FIGURE 17.3

Figure 17.4
3 vs. 3 WITH MEDIUM-LENGTH LONG BALL PLAYED TO CORNER GRID

This 3 versus 3 is about as complicated as a small-sided game should get. It combines a medium-length long ball out of pressure from the center channel to a winger in a corner grid with all-player movement in support of the pass and a finish on goal.

➤ Xs have possession.

➤ 3 versus 3 in a grid in the center channel.

➤ As soon as possible, play a long ball to one of the attackers in either corner grid.

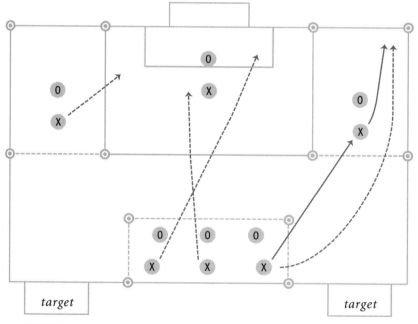

FIGURE 17.4

➤ Receiving player either takes her defender on in a 1 versus 1 to get to the goal line and cross or holds the ball and waits for an overlapping supporting attacker.

➤ Either way, as the ball reaches the goal line, all other players should be in an attacking position to receive the cross and make an attempt on goal; i.e., it is now a 6 versus 6 game to goal.

➤ As soon as possible, remove the grids at the outset and the exercise becomes a straightforward 6 versus 6 game initiated by a long ball from the center channel to the wide corner player, followed by effective supporting runs.

Coaching Points

➤ Attacking target corner players get separation from defenders to receive the ball.

➤ Central attackers and weak-side corner attacker make effective supporting runs.

➤ Defenders clear the ball to target goals on the halfway line.

Figure 17.5
3 vs. 3 WITH FULL-LENGTH LONG BALL PLAYED TO CORNER GRID ON OPPOSITE SIDE OF FIELD

This 3 versus 3 is similar to the previous game except that the medium-length long ball from the center channel to the corner grid is replaced with a true long ball from one side of the field to the other.

➤ Xs have possession.

➤ Same restrictions as in small-sided game 17.4 except the central 3 versus 3 grid is moved to one side; there are multiple variations on this game.

➤ The choice for the attacker on the ball is a shorter pass to the near-side corner grid to initiate a 1 versus 1, where the attacker can be supported easily by an overlapping support run.

➤ Another choice for the attacker on the ball is to play a long ball to the weak-side corner grid where the attacker is open; once the ball is passed, the central defender in front of the goal quickly closes the player down.

➤ Once the pass is made out of the initial 3 versus 3 grid, the game is live and becomes 5 versus 5 to the big goal.

Coaching Points

➤ As for small-sided game 17-4 except the choice is a long, accurate ball to an attacker with a defender playing off her on the weak side who is marking in advance, or a shorter pass to the near-side grid.

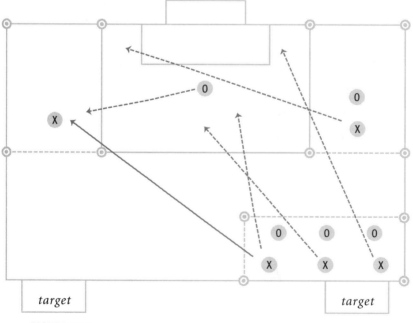

FIGURE 17.5

➤ An easier ball down the line to a forward who could be quickly supported, but where the defenders can more easily provide support for each other as well.

The Short Passing Game
and the 3 Plus 1

BECAUSE THIS BOOK CONTAINS a chapter expounding the virtues of the long ball and full-field vision, there must be a chapter on the short passing game as well. Despite the emphasis placed in this book on the long ball, the importance of the short passing game cannot be overemphasized. Its uses are many and varied, for example, setting up the long ball, breaking down packed defenses, or even maintaining possession to run down the clock on a hard-fought, narrow lead. The short passing game is used as a complementary tactic to the long ball offense, or as a complete alternative if the long ball offense gets closed down.

Sometimes the long ball is not available as the primary, initial attacking vehicle. The next option is to find a way to pull the defense either to one side of the field or toward the ball. This would set up the long ball switch across field, for example, or set up the long/medium ball into the corners or into space created by that compacting of the defense toward the ball.

In practice then, in emphasizing the short passing game, attention should be paid to implementing a long ball to complement the short ball. Small-sided games and restrictions on freegames should include a long ball element wherever possible, even when practicing short passing combination play.

This can be achieved even in simple warm-up exercises such as the small-sided game that follows. Figure 18.1 is a 2 versus 1 keepaway played in groups of five players, with two teams of two players and a neutral player. (See "Guide to Diagrams" on p. 89 for an explanation of the symbols.)

Figure 18.1
ROLLING 2 vs. 1 KEEPAWAY BETWEEN ADJACENT GRIDS

This small-sided game encourages short passing between players to maintain possession and then a longer ball to a supporting player, followed by a run by a neutral player in support of the longer ball.

➤ Xs have possession.

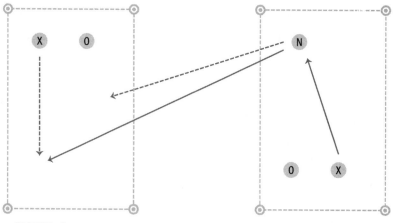

FIGURE 18.1

➤ In this small-sided warm-up keepaway game, there is a permanent 1 versus 1 game in each of two small adjacent grids.

➤ The two teammates in adjacent grids try to pass the ball to each other.

➤ A neutral attacking player follows the ball over from grid to grid, making a 2 versus 1 situation in whichever grid the ball is in. The neutral player is always on offense. Once one team loses the ball, the neutral player assumes a supporting attacking player role for the team now in possession.

➤ Change the neutral player every two minutes.

➤ The 2 versus 1 team has to make five passes together in their own grid before they can pass the ball to the other grid. Any player can pass the ball between grids.

Coaching Points

➤ Generate movement into space before the ball is passed in order to receive the ball and to relieve pressure.

➤ Generate movement after the pass in support of the ball carrier/receiver.

➤ Create separation from the defender by the receiving attacker in the other grid.

➤ Communicate with teammates.

Of vital importance to the use of a long ball in offense is movement off the ball by supporting attacking players while the compact-inducing short passing is going on, which creates the opportunity for such a long ball.

Ninety percent of what happens on a soccer field occurs off the ball. Movement off the ball establishes the opportunities for the ball carrier. Those on-the-ball opportunities run the gamut from dribbling with the ball, to scoring, to passing, to crossing.

In practice then, players should be encouraged to maintain constant movement in order to create opportunities on offense, whether looking for space to move into or dragging a marking defender out of position in order to create space for a teammate to exploit.

In this respect, the short ball passing game sets up the long ball. The short passing game focuses the defenders' attention on the ball and the immediate area around it. The short ball sucks players in and, if the defending team is not careful, creates a kind of mass tunnel vision with regard to covering "second" defenders and also "third" defenders farther from the action who are meant to be providing balance to the defense.

Coaches should have their teams practice the short passing game followed by the long pass, but without being too predictable! Coaches should not emphasize short-short-long all the time, highlighting instead the benefits of a long ball following a series of short passes. If a single short pass is enough to bring in a defender toward the ball and create space for another attacker to exploit, then a single pass is sufficient. Alternatively, if it takes four or five short passes to achieve the same effect—that is, directly or indirectly create space that can be exploited by the offense usually as a result of the defender's moving out of position—then that is how many should be used.

Again, one of the fundamental goals of the freegame philosophy is that coaches should encourage their teams to be unpredictable in their play on the field. A recipe for disaster is for a team to garner a reputation for being a slow-buildup, short passing type of team—unless of course they are also capable of playing offense using the accurate long ball and fast break. Get the opposition expecting one thing, and then play the other. That is also true for a team who plays offense using the accurate long ball and fast break. No matter how good the team is at attacking using the long ball out of defense, they will almost certainly eventually come face-to-face with a team that can effectively close that attack down. At that point, they also have to be capable of a short passing offense to break down that defense. You don't want attacking players standing still in the penalty box waiting for the cross; you always want them moving to arrive on the end of a cross at the same time as the ball in order to prevent the opposition from simply setting up a static defense. In the same way, an attacking team has to keep the defense on its toes, not letting the defense think it knows exactly how the offense is going to attack all the time.

In football, you need an effective running game to set up the passing game downfield. If all a team has is a running game, the opposition can bring numbers-up around the line of scrimmage to stop the run, knowing that only minimal coverage is necessary in the defensive backfield because of the lack of the long, accurate pass. It's the same for soccer; the threat of the long ball can create space for shorter passing combinations closer to the ball. And an effective short passing game creates opportunities and isolated defenders on the weak side of the field, away from the ball, that the accurate long ball can exploit.

But be aware that at the feet of unskilled players the long ball often results in a loss of possession. So coaches should not emphasize the long ball over unrealistic distances, bringing inaccuracy into play, just for the sake of using a long ball. Unfortunately for many players in the women's, and certainly the older girls' game, an accurate long ball translates into only a twenty-five-yard pass. That means linking long balls (really only medium-long balls) to switch the point of attack across the field is necessary to maintain effective possession. But the more passing links necessary to make the switch, the more time it takes to completely switch the point of attack, which translates into more time given the defense to slide over and cover the threat.

The short passing game is also extremely important in keeping the attack moving fluently along the flank into the attacking corner. Often the long ball to a winger playing wide up front will not be a realistic option; if the attacking team is playing with a wide front-running winger, a tight marking defender may make the long ball little more than a post-up, ball-holding position while support catches up. And often, that support is coming from either the outside midfielder or the center midfielder sliding over and pushing up from the center channel.

In an attack-oriented system, such as a 4-3-3, you want to be able to drop the long ball over the head of the winger into the attacking corner for her to run onto at speed and then cross. That is effective if the marking fullback is playing toward the inside of the attacker and a little way off. Sometimes though, that defender will be playing close to the attacker, will be playing over far enough to pick off the ball dropped into the corner, or be able to reach it before the attacker.

Alternatively, if the defense is playing with a sweeper or a tight zone, the supporting defender/sweeper may be able to slide over far enough to pick up any ball dropped into the corner. In that case, the long ball to that attacker may still be on if the defender is marking patiently goalside and is not willing to risk getting "turned" going in for the interception. In that instance the long ball should be to the feet of the attacker. It should not be dropped over her head for her to run onto, but placed to the outside of the target player, on the side away from the goalside marking defender.

What happens next depends on a number of factors: how accurate the ball is, how close the defender is marking, whether the attacker comes back for the ball and gains some separation from the defender, whether there is close attacking support to lay the ball off to and go for the return at speed, how quick the attacker can turn, how good a tackler the defender is, how good a dribbler the attacker is, and so on.

Front-running, wing-playing forwards are most likely to be seen these days in a 4-3-3 system of play or in the increasingly unlikely 4-2-4. In both systems the forward-playing winger is in an advanced position where she can check back to receive the long ball to the feet. In the more popular 4-4-2 system, where the advanced wing position is probably going to be filled by an advancing outside midfielder, the ball can be dropped into the corner space for the winger to run on to.

It can be argued that the long ball offense into the corners is more likely to have success and be the product of a 4-3-3 system, where three forwards are playing up most of the time.

In such a scenario, the advanced winger receiving the long ball to the feet finds her assigned defender between her and the goal. She should always have in mind what I call the "3 plus 1" initial series of options, of which the short passing game plays an important part.

The 3 Plus 1—Option 1

The first of the three passing options in the 3 plus 1 is after receiving the ball to the feet, the winger turns and plays the ball down the line. The player in the center-forward position makes a diagonal run toward the same-side corner flag in order to receive it or runs on to it (see figure 18.2). Xs are in possession.

The 3 Plus 1—Option 2

The second option in the 3 plus 1 involves a short passing combination that also ends up in the corner of the attacking third of the field (see figure 18.3). Simply put, the receiving winger holds the ball long

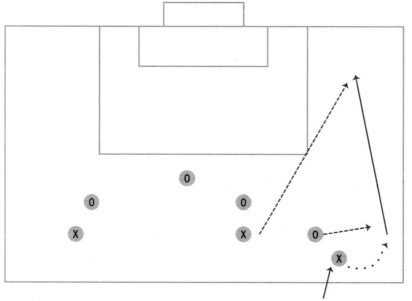

FIGURE 18.2   3 PLUS 1—OPTION 1

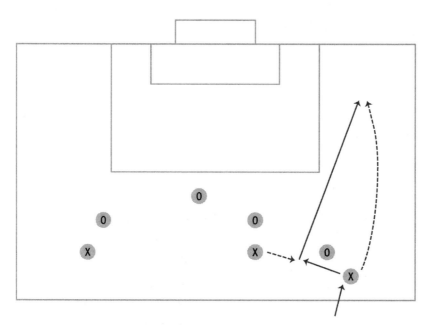

FIGURE 18.3   3 PLUS 1—OPTION 2

enough for the center forward to come over to receive a short pass inside. As soon as the winger plays the short pass inside to the center forward, she turns and sprints down the line toward the corner flag for the return ball from the center forward in a standard 1-2, give-and-go, or wall pass. Xs are in possession.

The 3 Plus 1—Option 3

The third option in the 3 plus 1 involves a long ball switch to the opposite-side corner in the event that the near-side corner is either closed down by the defense or doesn't offer as good as an attacking opportunity as the opposite side of the field (see figure 18.4). This option becomes especially attractive if the weak-side defender is playing a long way off the weak-side attacking winger (called "marking in advance" in zone defense terminology), thus giving that

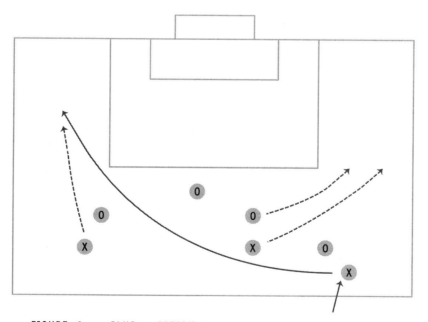

FIGURE 18.4 3 PLUS 1—OPTION 3

winger lots of space to receive the ball. It's also attractive if the sweeper has already been sucked into covering support too close to the ball. She has therefore left the opposite, weak-side corner without cover and left the weak-side fullback isolated 1 versus 1 with no effective covering defender (normally the sweeper in a nonzone defense). Xs are in possession.

The final "1" in the 3 plus 1 refers to the receiving player turning and dribbling the ball toward the goal in the event that the initial three passing options are not available.

The three passing options in the 3 plus 1 are preferable if only because passing the ball upfield moves the ball toward the opposition goal faster than dribbling, and because following a long ball out of the defensive third into the attacking third, most of the opposition players have as a result been caught on the wrong side of the quick long ball clearance.

But taking the defender on with the dribble depends on a variety of factors, all of which should have been considered by the winger before the ball is received, such as the winger's dribbling ability, her sprinting speed, the defender's patience, the defender's tackling ability, and the defender's speed, to name but a few.

If none of the 3 plus 1 options is available, the winger should act as a post-up target and simply maintain possession until a short/medium passing option becomes available courtesy of a supporting player, such as the center midfielder, outside midfielder, or attacking wingback advancing at speed from the outside fullback position. The most likely initial scenario though, following the closing down of all the elements in the 3 plus 1 option, will be a short/medium pass to a supporting player to set up the switching of the point of attack.

In addition to setting up the long ball or being used in short passing combinations to move the ball along the flank, the short passing game is also important as a way to break down a packed defense, such as a close-marking man-to-man system or tight zone. The keys to using the short passing game in breaking down such a defense are speed of passing (it has to be quick), movement by the supporting attacker to get into position as quickly as possible, movement by the ball carrier as soon as she makes the pass, vision by both the ball carrier and supporting attackers in order to spot the defensive weaknesses and spaces, technique to execute the passes usually under pressure, and accuracy in the passing for the receiving players to get the ball at their feet in order for the attack to continue quickly.

Uncomplicated small-sided games involving team passing in small areas are ideal for developing an effective and accurate short passing game. These can be with or without goals or targets and can often involve a simple possession game.

What follows are two more small-sided games that emphasize the short passing game. One is a simple possession game, and the other is a small-sided game involving goals.

Figure 18.5
3 vs. 3 TO SMALL GOALS

This is a physically demanding small-sided game played in a small area with multiple goals designed to encourage the use of the short passing game to create scoring chances. Maximum movement off the ball by supporting players is essential to maintain possession.

➤ 3 versus 3 in a small area; 4 small goals; no keepers.
➤ The better the players, the smaller the playing area.
➤ Using two small target goals at either end prevents defenders from simply setting up a static defense packed around a single central goal; they must slide over to defend both goals.
➤ Either play for a given amount of time or a set number of goals.

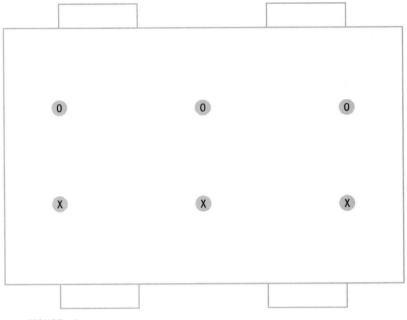

FIGURE 18.5

Coaching Points

➤ Generate movement before the ball is passed.

➤ Generate movement after the pass in support of the ball carrier.

➤ Communicate.

➤ The defending team must slide over from protecting one small goal to the other should the point of attack be switched.

Figure 18.6
SLIDING 4 vs. 4 POSSESSION GAME BETWEEN GRIDS

This small-sided game is a simple possession game between grids, with a long pass to the next grid following a series of short passes between teammates. The distance between grids can be large to encourage an accurate long ball and effective supporting runs between grids, to complement the short passing game.

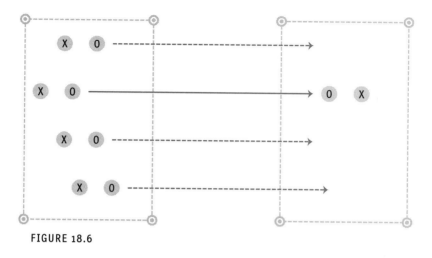

FIGURE 18.6

➤ Os have possession to start.
➤ 4 versus 4 or 3 versus 3 in one grid; 1 versus 1 in the other grid.
➤ Long ball to teammate in the other grid after five successful passes in the first grid.
➤ If 4 versus 4, then 3 attackers plus 3 defenders follow the ball into the other grid, creating another 4 versus 4 but this time in the other grid (leaving a 1 versus 1 in the original grid).
➤ Each successful long ball plus maintaining possession on the reception after the pass is worth a point.
➤ The better the players, the smaller the playing grids but the longer the distance between grids.

Coaching Points
➤ Generate movement before the ball is passed.
➤ Generate movement after the pass in support of the ball carrier.
➤ Communicate.
➤ Make an accurate long ball pass to 1 versus 1 grid.
➤ 1 versus 1 attacker must get separation from marking defender to receive ball and to maintain possession until support arrives.

Transition

Transition occurs when a team either loses possession of the ball, and therefore immediately goes from offense to defense, or wins possession of the ball, and therefore goes immediately from defense to offense.

Transition is probably the single most important moment in soccer. More games are won and lost in transition than at any other time.

Any team, at whatever level of play, has to be well versed with the moment of transition and practiced in their team response to its sudden development. A team unpracticed in defensive transition is going to lose a lot of games very quickly, while a team unpracticed in taking advantage of offensive transition opportunities is unlikely to create many goal-scoring chances.

Understanding fully both a team's defensive and offensive systems and style of play and each player's role in them is vital to all players if the team is to handle transition effectively.

For example, upon losing possession of the ball, the immediate transition to a zone defense can be very different from the transition to a straight man-to-man-with-sweeper marking defense. Players unsure of their team's defensive scheme and their role within it will be extremely ineffective in any fast-paced defensive transition.

Defensive Transition

Players have to know their role in their team's defensive scheme to contribute properly in the transition stage. By its very nature, just about every transition from offense to defense will be different, no matter how subtle. Thus defensive transition is best taught within the context of the freegame philosophy and free-flowing small-sided game.

Certainly patterns and shadow play will have their own role in the coaching and in the team's understanding of the situation. But the move to larger practice within the freegame concept should be as quick as possible. That said, however, no speedy move to the freegame should be at the expense of a complete understanding of the transition concept and the players' individual roles within it.

Once patterns and shadow play have been used to paint a suitable picture as to what is expected of individual players and what a team in transition should look like, the next stage is to move to free-flowing small-sided games emphasizing team transition, culminating in the effective execution in a full-field freegame environment.

A number of basic elements affect practicing transition: the size of the field, the number of players, and the team and tactical targets involved. So, while it can often be effective to begin coaching the transition at a small-numbered, smaller playing area level, coaches need to be aware that executing an effective transition game with 3 versus 3 in a small area is very different from executing it with 11 versus 11 on a full field.

The first necessity on defensive transition is to immediately apply pressure to the ball carrier. The nearest defender (upon loss of possession all eleven players become defenders) has to close down the space available to the ball carrier to make a forward pass. The ball carrier must be forced to delay her forward progress and the progress of the ball toward the goal.

Essentially, the first or nearest defender is gaining time for the defense to get into position. Without that delay, the job of the defense is that much harder, if not impossible.

So while the closest defender to the ball applies immediate pressure, and at least one more defender applies pressure to the closest supporting attacker, the rest of the defense backtracks toward their own goal to take up their positions. Where they go and how far back has to be determined by the coach before the game, and it has to be well practiced so all players become comfortable with their defensive roles.

Where the players go will be more preset in a zone defensive system than in a straight man-to-man system, where defensive positioning is to a great extent determined by where attacking players are moving.

But either way, the same basic rules usually apply: defenders should compact around the goal (tightly or loosely, depending on the predetermined approach), get between their marks and the goal (usually marking goal side and strong side wherever possible, to push passing lanes to the outside, away from goal), maintain defensive shape as much as possible (although that is really more important in zone defense than in a straight man-to-man defense), and be patient, both individually and as a team unit.

Compacting around the goal can be extreme, as in a tight zone defense where all zones on the strong side of the field where the ball is are filled with defenders. It can be loose, as in a straight man-to-man marking system where defenders are often required to follow their players around the field. And it can be a hybrid approach, a combination or compromise of the two.

Usually though, defenders should be aware that they can play off their mark when that player drifts into the weak-side zone and that they should avoid being pulled out toward the weak-side touchline. The latter can often result in attacking players' running through the center channel space vacated by the defender who has drifted outside to the weak side with her mark.

In the examples below, marking on the weak side should be as in figure 19.2, where the weak-side defender is playing off her mark, and not as in figure 19.1, where the weak-side defender is too close to her mark. (Xs are on offense in figures 19.1 and 19.2.)

In the man-to-man system examples seen here, figure 19.2 shows the weak-side defender playing off her mark in the weak side of the field and staying closer to the goal and the center channel to make herself available for any more immediate threat that may develop in that center channel.

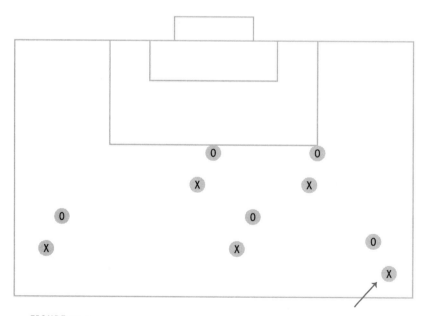

FIGURE 19.1

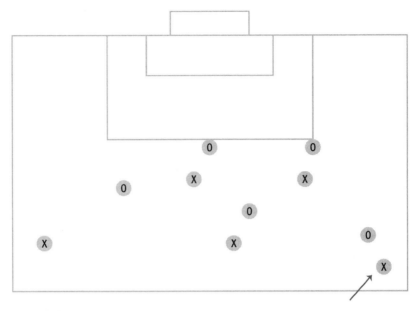

FIGURE 19.2

As with all defenders, or at least midfielders adopting a defensive role, players should be prepared to prioritize the various threats on goal. They need to be able to evaluate those threats and to go with whichever one presents the most dangerous scoring opportunity. Say a midfielder is marking an attacking player toward the weak side of the field and a fullback runs through the center channel without an accompanying marker and heads into the backfield toward the goal. The defending midfielder may have to leave her nonthreatening weak-side attacker and backtrack with the new attacking threat, the fullback, to make sure that player is marked up if no one is available among the defending fullbacks, or the sweeper if they are playing with one, to mark her. The original attacking player on the weak side in midfield is left alone until she presents a more direct threat to goal, at which time another defender will evaluate whether she is a more direct threat to the goal than her own mark and adjust accordingly. (See figure 19.3; Xs are on offense.)

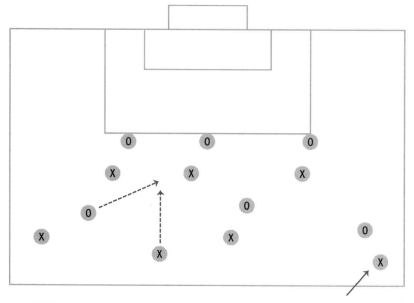

FIGURE 19.3

Soccer is the most fluid and constantly evolving team game in the world, and prioritizing the most immediate threat on goal and adjusting accordingly is a hugely important aspect of defending.

When backtracking to regain defensive shape upon loss of the ball upfield (in other words, when a team is in transition), defenders should be aware of where the ball is as well as where their assigned mark is in relation to the goal. This makes sound defensive sense in marking their players effectively. It also makes them available to counter any more immediate threat to goal. And it usually means the defender doesn't have to work so hard to get into the correct defensive position.

Teams will usually have a defensive line "drawn in the sand" behind which they will want to set up their defense upon transition. That line is rarely their own entire half of the field. It is more likely to be either the defensive third or somewhere around the midpoint between the halfway line and the defensive third line. Upon losing possession of the ball on the attacking side of the defensive line, the first defender and at least the second defender—that is, the two defenders closest to the ball—will apply pressure to the ball in order to delay its forward movement long enough for the defense to set up behind the defensive line.

The two players applying immediate pressure to the ball in defensive transition may not be forwards, just whoever is closest to the ball. That said, however, once the defense is set up behind the defensive line, it will usually be the forwards that apply pressure to the ball on the attacking side of the defensive line. And they need to apply pressure as a cohesive unit; this is true in any scenario,. If the team plays with three forwards, then those three forwards pressure the ball and the two supporting defenders closest to the ball carrier. If the team plays with two forwards, then there should be pressure on the ball carrier from one of them while the other applies simultaneous pressure to the second attacker, forcing a longer pass out of pressure or a backward pass.

With regard to defensive elements and shape, I have found that certain principles usually apply, including the following:

- Defenders should endeavor to keep the play in front of them and avoid getting caught on the wrong side of the ball.
- Whether marking zonally or straight man-to-man, defenders should usually stay strong side and goalside of their marks in order to force passing lanes to the outside and away from the goal.
- Generally there should be numbers-up on defense behind the ball.
- There should always be far more defenders in the strong-side zones than in the weak-side zones.

- Defenders must learn how to prioritize their defensive marking duties, to avoid an attacker coming through from the back and being allowed to roam unmarked in the penalty box.
- The defense will ultimately need to compact around the goal in some form in order to get between the most threatening and immediate attackers, as well as the ball, and the goal.
- Defenders must maintain a certain amount of defensive shape in order to have the required "pressure, cover, balance" trio of defenders, or at least have defenders in a position to offer immediate support to the first defender (the closest defender to the ball), whoever that turns out to be.
- The defense must be patient and avoid jumping in for the tackle.

Offensive Transition

Offensive transition is, for the most part, a mirror of defensive transition, and whatever elements are important in defensive transition, such as delay and compactness, need to be reversed.

For example, if defenders are initially seeking to delay the forward movement of the ball, it seems reasonable to impress on attacking players the need to immediately play the newly won ball upfield as fast as possible. This is in order to both catch as many attackers on the other team (now defenders) on the wrong side of the ball with an accurate long ball, and prevent the defense from quickly obtaining some sort of structured defensive shape.

That said, however, the loose, inaccurate long transition ball to a front-runner should not be at the expense of possession. There are times when a quick long ball out of defense is not advisable, even though such a ball should always be the first option considered. Risk is a fundamental element of the long ball offense, but it has to be a choice weighed against the need to keep a certain amount of possession out of the defensive third to alleviate constant pressure on goal and back into the defensive third.

The desire to create a numbers-up situation on offense in the attacking third with the long transition ball must be tempered with a certain degree of restraint. Such a ball may carry with it the high possibility of an immediate loss of possession and the ball's being played back into the defending third before the defense even has the chance to push up and out of penalty box pressure.

With regard to immediate offensive transition then, width, as opposed to defensive compactness, is a primary attacking tool. Upon gaining possession of the ball, defenders should immediately either look to pass the ball to the outside channels or look to run toward the outside touchline in order to offer themselves as a passing option should the long transition ball to a front-runner not be viable.

Whether in transition or not, the outside option is an indispensable attacking tool anywhere on the field, whether the defensive third, the middle third, or the attacking third.

But the outside option stands to be even more successful in the attacking transitional stage—providing the more direct pass is not a viable option. There defenders must think fast and are often conditioned by drills to think too one dimensionally with regard to compacting, backtracking, reaching the defensive line, and maintaining some sort of close-support defensive team shape favoring the strong side of the field or, more likely, the center channel.

Such a knee-jerk defensive reaction to the loss of possession can often open up opportunistic attacking possibilities with regard to the outside option and wing play.

Essential elements of such opportunistic transitional play include the following:

- the speed with which attacking players can move outside and become a passing option.

- how quickly the ball can be played forward
- the speed at which the attack can cross the opposition's defensive line before the defense has a chance to set up properly, which takes them out of their defensive comfort zone
- the weak-side penetration of attacking players, preferably fullbacks and wingbacks

With regard to practicing transitional play, activities should be used in which both the defensive and offensive transitional game can be addressed at the same time. Small-sided games with increasing numbers of players, with different types of targets, and using a variety of restrictions can be used to teach the fundamental elements of transitional play. As always, the short-term goal is to move to a full field as quickly as possible, but not at the expense of a full understanding of the fundamental elements of the transition stage.

What follows are four transition small-sided games, beginning with a 3 versus 3 and progressing in numbers and levels of complexity until all essential elements of transition have been addressed. (See "Guide to Diagrams" on p. 89 for an explanation of the symbols.) While complexity is an element that needs to be included in any evolving series of small-sided games, the golden freegame coaching rule "Keep it simple" should not be sacrificed.

Figure 19.4
3 vs. 3 TO A SINGLE BIG GOAL

This great small-sided game is designed to encourage defenders to stay goalside and on the strong side relative to their marks, so any passing lanes flow away from the goal and not toward it.

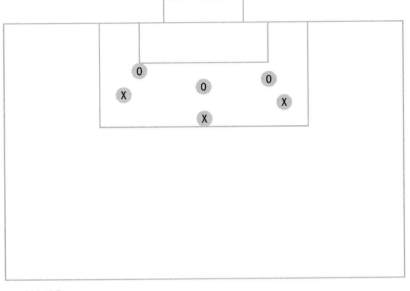

FIGURE 19.4

➤ Xs have initial possession.
➤ 3 versus 3 to a single big goal in a medium-sized grid.
➤ No keeper.
➤ Score by walking the ball across the goal line.
➤ No dribbling around a defender.
➤ Pass only to get by a defender.
➤ On loss of possession (immediate transition), offense becomes defense and defense becomes offense.

Coaching Points
➤ Defenders stay on the strong side, goalside, forcing passing lanes away from the goal.
➤ Be patient in defense; don't jump into the tackle.
➤ Generate movement in offense before and after pass.
➤ Offensive players to get separation from their markers.

Figure 19.5
4 vs. 4 TO BIG GOAL PLUS TWO SMALL GOALS

This small-sided game is designed to keep attacking players aware of their
immediate defensive responsibilities upon loss of possession. The two goals
at one end mean that the attacking team cannot simply pack the center
channel upon transition, but must work together to defend effectively.

➤ Xs have initial possession.

➤ 4 versus 4 to big goal, two small goals.

➤ One side defends the big goal with a keeper; switch after a few
   attempts to score.

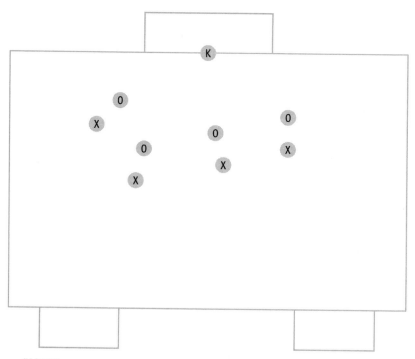

FIGURE 19.5

➤ Attacking team defends two small goals with no keepers in outside channels upon losing possession.

➤ Upon loss of ball in open play, attacking team immediately defends two small goals, sliding left and right as needed depending on which goal is threatened.

➤ Added element: no dribbling by a defender (attackers have to pass to get by), or a freegame with no restrictions.

Coaching Points

➤ Move the ball across field quickly when attacking the two small goals to switch the point of attack.

➤ Defense must concentrate on communication when attacking the two small goals.

➤ Compact around the big goal on defense and be patient in stopping the shot.

Figure 19.6
3 vs. 3 *or* 4 vs. 4 TO TWO BIG GOALS

This small-sided game combines a number of elements already discussed in this book, all within the context of transition play. Upon gaining possession of the ball, the attacking side must play the ball out to the wingers in order to create a scoring chance.

➤ 3 versus 3 or 4 versus 4 in a medium-sized playing area (size depends on players' abilities) with two outside channels marked with cones.

➤ Two big goals with keepers at either end.

➤ Neutral player in each outside channel used only on offense.

➤ Score only directly from a cross from the neutral player.

➤ Added element: have 1 versus 1 in the outside channel instead of neutral players.

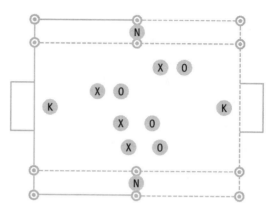

FIGURE 19.6

Coaching Points

➤ Immediate transition upon ball turnover.

➤ Generate movement before and after the ball is passed.

➤ Defensive fundamentals—get between your mark and the goal, be patient, provide support, maintain compactness.

➤ Offensive fundamentals—use width, use speed in getting ball forward, develop ability to lose marker.

➤ Utilize crossover runs in front of the goal to gain space for shot.

Figure 19.7
4 vs. 4 TO SMALL GOALS

This small-sided game is played on a relatively small area to encourage maximum scoring chances and therefore a quick turnover of teams. The goals should be close enough that upon loss of possession, the attacking team can immediately be within scoring distance. Being so close, however, means that defenders are also close, which makes short, quick passes necessary to create the shooting space.

➤ 4 versus 4 in an open freegame in a medium-sized playing area
   (3 teams of 4 players).

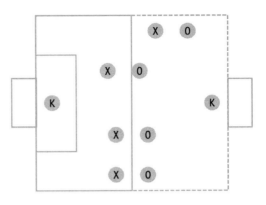

FIGURE 19.7

➤ Two big goals with keepers.
➤ The team missing on shot leaves the field; scoring team stays on.
➤ Immediate transition upon ball turnover.
➤ Added element: three players must touch the ball before shooting.
➤ Added element: two-touch or one-touch.

Coaching Points

➤ Use width quickly on attacking transition, but a longish ball forward the first option.
➤ Generate movement before and after the pass.
➤ Defense must be patient and not jump in.
➤ Defense must compact around the goal and stay on the strong side, goalside.

A Typical Practice Session

PART OF THE PREMISE OF this book is that there should be no typical practice. Each practice should be dictated in large part by the players themselves and should therefore include a healthy dose of spontaneity. The coach should be able to think on his or her feet, integrating coaching points that need to be worked on into the practice as it moves along.

But in order to help you visualize the freegame "hands-off" coaching philosophy, this chapter features a "typical" practice example. A simple flow chart at the end of the chapter may also help your understanding of the concept.

As mentioned, in the women's game, establishing and maintaining a comfortable practice environment is extremely important. It's the foundation from which the coach can challenge players' abilities and character. Make them feel comfortable and then periodically take them out of that comfort zone and test them as the practice session or training calls for it.

So initially, then, the task is to establish a comfortable working environment.

Here, I should reiterate a coaching philosophy point. The coach is part of the team, not some demigod handing down instructions from a high pedestal. So it is important that the coach be prepared to invest what I would call "sweat equity" in the team. Sweat equity doesn't have to actually entail engaging in physical activity, although that would be preferable. My own feeling is that a coach should at least be capable of demonstrating, even with limited ability, a technique or activity that the team is to do.

But sweat equity can take other forms. The coach should make sure that the team members get to the field early and have everything set up in advance, for example. If a team is using colored bibs, then the coach can make sure the bibs are washed for each practice. A visual demonstration of a coach's sweat equity is required; players need to see the coach is taking the commitment seriously and is willing to invest effort as well as time. Making sure there is water on hand for everyone by physically carrying the water cooler onto the field is one example.

Warm-ups should be inclusive, interactive, and, wherever possible, made up of exercises and stretches chosen by the players. Warm-ups could consist of a ten-minute jog with periodic stops for stretching. The coach can run with the players if he or she is able. At each stop a player may suggest a stretch that the team can do. Most older players would have been playing soccer for many years, stretching at each practice with all manner of different teams and coaches, so knowing stretches to suggest is not the problem for most of them; it is feeling comfortable enough to suggest them.

Again, creating a comfortable environment in which players are willing to suggest stretches and team activities is very important.

Getting all the players involved helps to create free-thinking individuals who will be creative and unpredictable on the field of play, players who are not always looking to the sideline for coaching directions.

After the jog and stretches, in which the coach is involved, players might be asked to suggest other warm-ups, such as ball control activities. As long as the activities warm up all the necessary parts of the body, any activities suggested will serve the correct purpose. And letting them make suggestions creates a feeling of inclusiveness and team unity.

It is common practice among coaching organizations in the U.S. to teach coaches that warm-up activities should relate to the coaching points being covered during the ensuing practice. Why? It looks good on paper. But again, especially for women, the coach should be trying to create a comfortable practice environment for the players. They must enjoy their practice time and have fun, because they are training so much and, if nothing else, a happy team is much easier to motivate than an unhappy team.

Next, let's talk! No really, let's talk. At least let women players talk. The social aspects of team association are extremely important for women, much more so than men, although some would argue it is also required in the men's game if the team is to be successful on the field.

But for women and girls at all levels, the social element is vitally important. So coaches should encourage players to socialize, at least in the initial phase of a regular practice and maybe while warm-ups are going on, or until the serious work requiring concentrated focus comes around. Emphasize to the players that as long as they warm up and stretch properly, they may socialize and have nonsoccer conversations if they want. But if their performance warm-ups or initial ball control activities appear to be lacking, then the socializing may have to stop.

But remember that heavy-handed coaching and ultimatums rarely work effectively with the female player and can drive a wedge between the players and the coach.

After the team has warmed up—using many of the ball-control activities that the players have chosen themselves—and, more important, have had their fifteen minutes of socializing, it's time for a freegame.

The coach then just divides up the squad into two equal teams, hands out two sets of colored bibs, sets up two goals with keepers, and lets them have a freegame for ten to fifteen minutes.

Players don't become part of a soccer team to be coached. They join a team to play the game. And in many cases for women, they also join to have social interaction with others their own age with similar interests. So I advocate letting them play a freegame at the beginning of practice.

As mentioned in Chapter 1, coaches almost universally will dangle that promise of a freegame at the end of practice in front of players; if the players behave themselves and do what the coach says then they get ten minutes of freegame at the end of a two-hour practice. But by that time the players are all tired. So where's the fun in letting them have a freegame at the end of practice? If they have a freegame, not a long one, at the beginning of practice they'll have some fun and remember why they're giving up all the other social activities that their friends are engaged in in order to be on a soccer team.

They want to play soccer, so I say let them play. If they get it out of their systems the practice can move on and they can concentrate on what the coach is trying to teach.

So the practice moved from a jog and stretching, to some warm-up ball control activities, to a ten- to fifteen- minute freegame with no restrictions.

The next step is for the coach to demonstrate the technique or tactical element to be emphasized in the practice.

Demonstrating is extremely important in soccer. Again, in demonstrating, wherever possible, the coach should use players as examples. Usually there will be at least one or two players that can demonstrate the technique as well as the coach. But if the coach wants to lead by example, then he or she should by all means do so.

The next step is to explain in depth the place or the role of the technique or tactical play in the overall game and how it relates to the team.

By nature, women are far more curious about how things fit into the overall picture than men. Young teenagers to players in their late twenties all want an explanation of how they will use whatever it is that the coach is teaching. This can be a little disconcerting and tiring for a soccer coach used to coaching the males, who most of the time are just happy with a quick demonstration in order to speed up getting out on the field.

Do not underestimate the importance of a good, thorough explanation of the subject matter and how it fits in with the overall picture to women. Also, coaches must be prepared to answer questions on how the theory can be applied tactically as well. And the more female players feel comfortable with the coach and the practice environment, the more questions they will likely ask.

Coaches must embrace the curiosity! It is often what makes coaching women's soccer so interesting and fulfilling. And it'll keep good coaches on their toes intellectually.

After the demo and explanation of how the subject fits into the entire picture, it is time to break up into freegames again, only this time to apply the theory in a game environment. The coach should tell the players that the idea is for them to apply the theory. If it's overlapping runs that are being worked on, then the coach needs to tell them that they must use overlapping runs before the practice can move on to the next stage.

Whenever possible, it is useful to break the squad of players up into 5-a-side games—maybe two games at once for a squad of twenty. For smaller squads maybe two 4-a-side games would work. The idea is to have small-numbered freegames initially so all players get more touches on the ball and are involved in the game throughout its duration.

And here's an important part of freegame coaching and in my coaching philosophy of empowering players to excel and to learn from other players. There will almost always be a couple of players that do the technique, or whatever is being practiced, very well— the overlap, for example. The coach must make sure those two players are on the same team in the 5-a-side game and at the earliest convenient opportunity, when they have just carried out a good example of the overlap, stop both games. This is the time for the coach to explain that theirs is a good example of how the overlap should be accomplished and have them repeat the overlap that they just carried out in the game.

With the empowering demonstration finished, the two games continue. I would argue that if a picture is worth a thousand words and a good demo from the coach is worth two thousand, then a good demo from players is worth at least double that.

Players will learn from players. But much more than that, many women and older teenage girls like it when a teammate is singled out as an example of excellence. And a good player demo will inspire all the other players to concentrate and try just a little bit harder. The coach should attempt to spread the praise and the good examples around among all players. Inclusiveness is one of the keys to successfully coaching female players.

Now, as can be seen by the flow chart at the end of this chapter, if the small-numbered freegame works (for example, 5 versus 5) and players can apply the theory in the small-numbered game in which they get a lot of touches and space is limited, it is time to make the leap to a full-field freegame. The coach needs to explain again that the idea is for the players to apply the theory, only this time in the context of a full game.

Of course, what I have described, a practice in which players pick up the technique or element of the game from the coach or player demo and can apply it to a real game, is the best-case scenario. And because this is women's soccer it is often the case.

But in moving to the small-numbered freegame it is sometimes evident that the players are going to need some help in applying the theory to actually what happens out on the field.

Initially then, still within the small-numbered freegame, the coach should implement a single restriction to make the players start focusing on how they are to apply the theory.

Here's an example utilizing one of my favorite restrictions: If the coaching point is to encourage the first passing option to always be forward, enforce a restriction on the game that there are to be no square or backward passes; everything has to go forward. Obviously, there are times when a forward pass is likely to cause loss of possession, in which case a square or backward pass is the only realistic option. But the forward-pass-only restriction on the freegame helps the players get into the proper "We have the ball so we're attacking" frame of mind.

As with all coaching tools, freegame restrictions should be used for a short time, maybe ten minutes, before the restriction is changed or a second one is added. A coach needs to challenge the players intellectually and have them focus on a specific element of the game, but not get them into the habit of thinking with tunnel vision.

If it becomes apparent that a single restriction on the freegame is not working and the players are failing to adequately implement the technique or element of the game that was demonstrated, then it is time to either change the restriction to a different one or add a second restriction.

Sometimes just changing the restriction to a different one can be all that's needed to jump-start a team's understanding of how to apply a certain lesson in a freegame. Maybe a variation of the original restriction is all that is needed, or maybe a complete change to a different type is necessary.

I would be wary of using more than two restrictions at once in a freegame. The idea behind restrictions in a freegame is to focus players on a particular element in their play, not make the game so complicated that their soccer suffers because they are trying to remember the rules of engagement.

As much as possible, coaching tools should be as simple as possible. Players should be intellectually challenged, of course, but too much "artificial" or coaching-induced cerebral activity can negatively impact on their ability to play effective soccer in a real game situation.

Often, playing with two restrictions is enough before moving on to some other coaching tool such as a top-down progression.

In other words, the coach should move to the freegame with a single restriction, and if that doesn't work, either add a second restriction to the first or go to a completely different restriction.

If that second restriction is still not working, then there are two options: either take a break, or move to a second coaching tool, such as a top-down progression. Taking a break could involve literally a water break coupled with a discussion with the players as to why the activity is not working. Maybe they still don't understand what is expected of them or how the demo is suppose to apply to the real game.

After the break, the practice should either move to a top-down progression, for example, or return to a small-sided freegame with or without a restriction for another attempt at implementation.

And, as always, your rule as a coach would be "Know your players." You should be the best person to judge whether just returning to a freegame with or without restrictions after another explanatory talk is going to work. You must know your players in detail. And that's because one size does not fit all in soccer, especially in the women's game. What works for one coach and one team does not necessarily work for another.

Know your players and adjust your coaching accordingly. Don't go into a coaching session with a set-in-stone practice already written up on the dreaded clipboard, with blinders to the needs of the players.

A next stage then, with the players having failed to apply the theory adequately in a restricted and nonrestricted freegame, could be to move on to a top-down progression.

Depending on the players and their intellectual and technical abilities, a coach can choose to begin at the top level or any level below that. But the entire premise behind the top-down progression—and this book—is that, because women players are generally more cerebral and have a better intellectual grasp of what is expected of them, it is probably not necessary to go to the lower levels.

I would expect most women's teams to be able to start at either the top level in a progression, multiple players in a gamelike situation going to a big goal with a keeper; or the next level below the top level, such as a numbers-up offense going to a small goal without a keeper but with defenders.

Of course what constitutes the second level from the top depends on how the coach structures the progression in the first place. Some coaches define that second level as a much more fundamental stage and have a full defense, even an outnumbered one, competing for the ball only at the top level.

Either way, the idea is to explain the reason for the practice and what is expected of the players and then proceed into the initial stage of the top-down progression: top level, second from top, or even third from top.

The principle is the same wherever you start. If the players still fail to grasp the concept at the initial stage, drop down to the next level and try again. If they fail again, the coach can either drop it down one more stage or take alternative action.

I personally am not one for flogging a dead horse! If at this stage players are still having trouble, I think it may be time for a complete change. So the practice should move on to something else and come back to that coaching point either later in the same practice, utilizing the same or different activities, or in another practice session, maybe the following day. There are many times a team just needs to ponder a problem away from the field before they click on its application in the real game.

Either way, it's best to avoid getting bogged down in practice trying to force home a coaching point when it's pretty obvious the players are not going to understand it, at least that day. Before moving on though, the coach should explain to the team that they didn't grasp it properly and another practice session will address the problem after they've had time to think about it.

Finally, whether they have grasped the concept or not, if they have been working hard it's always a good idea to finish with a freegame with no restrictions for the last ten minutes of practice. Players belong to a team because they want to play, so let them play.

Always finish practice on a happy or positive note. A freegame perhaps, or something else competitive, even a penalty competition or a heading contest, but something that will remind them why they love to play the game. This is even more important to both team and individual player morale if the session has been hard or they have failed to grasp the coaching concept that has been worked on.

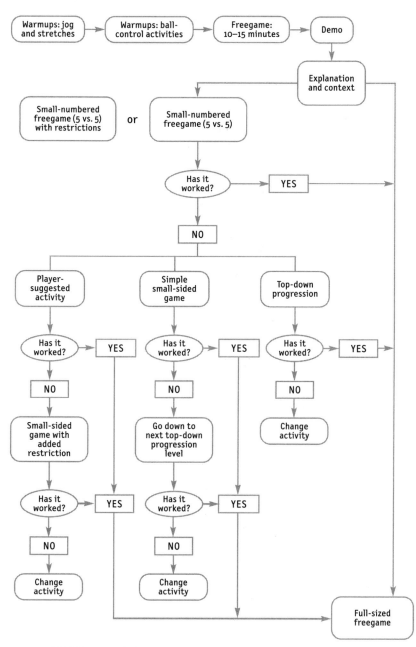

FIGURE 20.1 TYPICAL PRACTICE

A Few Final Thoughts

FOR MOST PLAYERS AND coaches, playing and practicing with the freegame as the focal point may be unfamiliar territory. But hopefully in this book I have shown that using the freegame doesn't just mean "no coaching." It is simply a different way of coaching - more player-centric and open.

My philosophy of coaching has less formal structure. But it still has structure—it's just better disguised. It is much more demanding on coaches but, most important, it is much more rewarding for players, as they become part of the process instead of just followers of a coach's clipboard practice scheduling. There is less for a coach to hide behind, but there can be more resources from which to draw—that is, the players.

I've coached at almost every level of soccer, from Under 6 recreational through girls and boys Under 17 state Olympic Development Program and up into the college level. An open coaching style, such as I have described in this book, receives an enthusiastic response from female players, wherever I have utilized it. But it may take you time to fully develop, depending on how unused to it and how over-drilled the players are from previous coaches.

The game will teach. And players will learn from players. Coaches should create positive soccer environments within which female players can learn, explore, and experiment. And open, creative practices will eventually give rise to better empowered and increasingly spontaneous players seeking to duplicate that openness and creativity on the soccer field in pressure competition.

Impending games, time constraints, and schedules notwithstanding, at all other times of the year, an open, freegame-oriented style of coaching will pay dividends in both player and team development, as well as players' feelings of inclusiveness and camaraderie.

I might add that such an open coaching style will also make all coaches better coaches—at every level of play.

Index